TO LIVE IS TO LOVE

TO LIVE IS TO LOVE

ERNESTO CARDENAL

Translated by Kurt Reinhardt

HERDER AND HERDER

1972
HERDER AND HERDER NEW YORK
232 Madison Avenue, New York 10016

Nihil obstat: Leo J. Steady, Censor Librorum
Imprimatur: † Robert F. Joyce
Burlington, October 6, 1971

ISBN 665-00002-2
Library of Congress Catalog Card Number: 70-178873
© 1972 by Herder and Herder, Inc.
Manufactured in the United States

Contents

Introduction

BY THOMAS MERTON

In a time of conflict, anxiety, war, cruelty and confusion, the reader may be surprised that this book is a hymn in praise of love, telling us that "all beings love one another."

Perhaps we are too much used to saying that one *ought* to love (thereby giving to understand that, generally speaking, we do not love). We know that there is a *duty* to love, that men have received a *commandment* to love each other. But we take it for granted that they hardly ever obey this commandment. And thus we conclude that the world is evil because there is so little love in it, and we blame and castigate those whom we hold responsible for this lack of love.

Thus a theology or ethics of punishment and retribution takes the place of the vision of love, and love becomes an idealized abstraction. The daily reality of our lives is not under the rule of love, but under the rule of law, of force and of punishment. We talk about love, but we live by hate: we hate in the name of love. In this situation it becomes necessary to assert once more that to love is *not* impossible. Love is not something unreal. On the contrary, love is the *only* reality. Everything that is, is by virtue of love, and if love is not clearly evident in all things, the reason is that we ourselves have made no effort to *see* love in all things. In a very radical sense, love is the only and unique possibility. And everything that is not love is essentially and basically impossible.

The purpose of this book is quite simply to open our eyes to what ought to be obvious but sounds incredible: that "all beings love one another," that "all life is love." This book therefore does not say that men ought to love, nor does it lament the fact that actually men do not love. It does not tell us in great detail how men should be punished for their failure to love. It simply tells us that all things love one another, and it adds that, as a matter of fact, men do love, whether they know it or not. It asserts that men can never cease loving. Even the atheist loves God, unbeknown to himself. If men live in discord with each other and with God, it is not because they do not love, but because they do not understand and accept the fact that they are bound to love of necessity.

Psychoanalysis has taught us that much hate and fear, and even many physical illnesses, are caused by a love which refuses to acknowledge itself as such, a love which has become ill because it fails to recognize its true nature and has lost sight of its object. The conflicts which beset our world are not caused by the absence of love, but by a love which no longer recognizes itself, a love which has become disloyal to its own reality. Cruelty is misdirected love, and hate is frustrated love.

The lucid and "Franciscan" simplicity of Father Cardenal shows us the world not as we see it, with fear and distrust in our hearts, but as it is in reality. Love is not a dream. It is the basic law of all those creatures who were created free in order to give themselves to others, free to partake of the infinite abundance of life with which God has filled our being. Love is the heart and the true center of that creative dynamism which we call life. Love is life itself in its state of maturity and perfection.

The saints were capable of seeing through the masks that cover the faces of humanity, and they saw that the masks are unreal. In the innumerable faces of men they saw only one face:

the face of love (that is to say, the face of Christ). This is what Ernesto Cardenal has seen and written down. His entire book is an ever-repeated discovery, an ever new poetic intuition of the central reality of life. It is a hymn to life, and this is why it is so eminently truthful. With the depth of conviction Cardenal speaks again and again of that which simply *is*. *Love is.* All else *is not,* because in the same measure in which things partake of being, they partake of love. All that is not love, *is not.* All that which is, has its being and its action in love.

Non-rational creatures are guided by a love which they do not know, toward an end which they do not understand. For the animal lives in nature without being conscious of it and without that freedom which is the gift of conscious existence. The animal lives immersed in life, a life without reflection. We might therefore say that the animal is "animated" by life and by love in a passive manner and without being cognizant of it. The animal has no other choice than this "being animated" by its own nature.

This, as Rainer Maria Rilke said in the *Duino Elegies,* is the reason why the animal is always in immediate contact with life. Consciousness never intervenes between the animal and life. The animal never reflects on life but simply *lives,* and living is its only way of knowing. The animal does not recognize itself as being alive; it simply lives what it cognizes.

The gift of consciousness is a divine blessing, but it may turn into a curse if we do not want it to be a blessing. If consciousness, as Rilke saw it, were a pure consciousness of love, our love would be as immediate and spontaneous as life itself. As the animal is "animated" immediately and directly by the life of nature, so we should be activated and motivated in the inwardness of our consciousness by supernatural and divine love. Our consciousness

9

would then not be dimmed by a feeling of frustration, on account of our limitations. It would be a pure consciousness of love, of God, and of life as a gift of love.

The human person, however, is not merely "animated" or "vitalized" by its nature. The person is autonomous, conscious of itself, capable of betraying its nature (even though incapable of changing it) and thus capable of either affirming or denying its nature. Man is capable of being or becoming human, whether he likes it or not. He is capable of being a son of God with the full consent of his will or contrary to his will. He can accept himself or reject himself. He is capable of loving his fellow men freely, spontaneously, with complete overtness, or he may prefer to reject and despise them, and in this case he will still love them, even though contrary to his own will. He will love them unknowingly. Thus, even though he still loves, his love has turned against his own self. It has become adulterated, contaminated and disingenuous. That love with which, in the depth of his heart, man wants to open himself to others, turns in upon himself and is locked up inside himself. The love which could and should give nourishment to others, consumes itself. The love which should have found its full realization in self-giving, founders in the confusion and the torment of negation. And it is ironic that negation often hides under the name of love.

Creation in its totality could teach man how to love if only he were willing to accept its teaching. Life as such is love, and if it is lived in truth, it teaches us to love. But when man's consciousness has been corrupted by the rejection of love, man, who is God's creature, remakes the world in his own image, and the result is a world filled with cruelty, greed, hate, fear and strife. If, on the other hand, man consents to love and gives himself over to life in its pristine purity—life as a pure gift of God—the entire world is overflowing with love.

Isaac of Stella, a Cistercian mystic of the twelfth century, writes:

"This visible world serves man, its master, in two ways: it nourishes him and it teaches him. As a good servant, the world nourishes and teaches, provided that man be not a bad master. A bad master is stupid and wretched; his eyes may be able to penetrate with their glance to the ends of the world and yet see nothing but darkness, and he will then make the world subservient to his body and his stomach. He has no longer any idea why the world was created. He believes that this immense universe was made by God for the sake of his small belly."

Isaac of Stella was surely aware of the meaning and importance of nourishment, and he was familiar with the joys of festive meals. God has given himself to us in the eucharistic meal, so that man might be capable of communion with God in the gifts of the earth and the fruits of his labor. Isaac knows of the pleasures of wine and of festivity, but he is aware that these are only images of the sublime joy of that love by which God gives to us his Spirit like a "torrent of delight that inebriates us with a fervor of charity." Love is for Isaac that divine wine which intoxicates and enraptures us. God wants us to drink of this wine, but we are afraid to do so, notwithstanding His continuous invitation.

This book is filled with invitations to drink and to delight in the banquet of love. Or, to say it much better, it invites us to open our eyes and look at the world around us, so that we may recognize that the festive meal is right in front of us, that the wine, unbeknown to us, is within the reach of our hand.

These basic principles illuminate for us both the creative dynamism of nature and the refreshing and redeeming dynamism of grace. However, these simple principles cannot be acquired in the splendid tepidity of abstract meditation. These

11

pages are filled with the concrete firmness of conviction, because the author wrote them after having completely surrendered to love when he entered a strictly contemplative monastic community, far away from his homeland. Love has its seat not only in the mind or in the heart; it is more than mere thought and desire. Love is action, and it is only in the action of love that we attain to the contemplative intuition of loving wisdom. This contemplative intuition is an act of the highest degree and kind; it is the purest kind of love. And this love does away with the apparent contradiction between action and contemplation.

In order to attain to such a mature act of love, we must first have experienced contradiction and conflict. Love is the pinnacle of freedom and of a fully personalized consciousness. And love discovers its own being only in the act of love. A love which acts without being fully conscious of its action, acts contrary to its very nature and does not attain to a full consciousness of self. It remains, as it were, in hiding before itself. Nor is it capable of acting perfectly in accordance with its own nature. The one who acts remains then somehow separated from his love, and his action does not measure up to the fullness of his love. Love here is in contradiction with itself. It rules the heart with a strange and oppressive passion. It carries with it bitterness, anxiety, repression, violence, and even a taste of death. For every love that is not a totally free and spontaneous self-giving, harbors a taste of death. This means then that all our love—the love of us average human beings, who are neither saints nor mystics—is beset with contradiction, conflict and bitterness. And it carries with it a taste of death.

What shall we say of this kind of love? That it should not be? That it is sinful? That it should not be permitted or should be punished? Alas, it is surely true that our poor love tastes of sin. However, Ernesto Cardenal says of it simply that it is *love*, but a love that is not yet sufficiently free, not yet sufficiently pure. And we might add that by what it lacks in being true love we may discover the way that leads to true and perfect love. It is by *accepting this imperfect love, fully conscious of its imperfection, that our love may be made perfect.*

The first step on the way to true and perfect love is the admission that our love, even though not yet pure, is nonetheless love and that by virtue of its very nature it aspires to become pure.

Our moralists sometimes tell us that what is needed is justice, righteousness, honesty, truth and love; that there should be no room for egotism, iniquity and injustice; that egotism should be eradicated and love should be made obligatory.

For the moralist human life is a complex system of virtues and vices, and love is assigned a definite place in the system; it is one of the several virtues. However, the mystic knows of no such complex system; for him love is the one and the all. For him the virtues are different aspects of love, and he holds that the same is true of the vices. The virtues are manifestations of a love that is alive and hale. And the vices are symptoms of an enfeebled love, of a love which refuses to be what it is in its essence.

Actually there is nothing else but love. But this love may live in contradiction with itself. It may at one and the same time be love and hate, love and greed, love and fear, love and envy, love and lust. It is destined, however, to be simply love, without any self-contradictory admixture. And love cannot fulfill its true destiny if we merely try to suppress our hatreds, our greeds, our fears, our jealousies, our lusts. These evil forces receive their strength solely from love. To suppress them is to suppress love. On the contrary, these evil drives ought to be made fully conscious of themselves as love in disguise, and if this is the case, they will not be able to divert the potency of love to the service of that which is not love.

This means that the root of evil and of moral infirmity is

13

ignorance with regard to the kind of love which fails to recognize its true identity and which is therefore blind with respect to its true being and its strength. In the measure in which love begins to become conscious of itself, it recognizes its self-betrayal. It is confused by the spectacle of its radical inner discord. It is frightened by the sight of its divided self and thus becomes the prey of great anguish. For this reason a feeble love prefers to remain unconscious of itself or to know itself only in the form of some disguise. In the degree to which it becomes conscious of itself, it becomes conscious of its inherent contradictions. And thus all our conventional love, if we dare face it, recognizes itself as impure, anguished, divided and burdened with suffering. Such a love is therefore a veritable agony, in the original sense of this term—a tremendous *struggle*. Although God wanted life to be a pure consciousness of love and peace, it is actually a fierce struggle, because in our actual human existence, life is the agony of a love which fears to accept itself, aware of the fact that it is self-contradictory, self-affirmation and self-negation at one and the same time. "He who lives in constant struggle lives in agony, fighting against life itself," wrote Unamuno.

This, then, is the central problem of every human love. Regardless of how pure love may be, our love is divided by an inherent self-contradiction as long as we are weak human beings, living on this earth and in time. Our love repulses and negates itself. Only God's love is perfectly pure. And human love can only approximate that divine purity in the mystic or the saint who is wholly filled with the love of God. All others (including the one who may some day become a mystic but is not one yet) are bound to live in the anguish of contradiction, or perhaps to be content with a love that is not fully conscious of itself. We experience in ourselves the anguish of this inner conflict from the moment we

14

begin to love. To accept love into our conscious life is to accept simultaneously the consciousness of our agony.

The basic contradiction which love has to face is the contradiction between life and death. A false religious idealism imagines sometimes that it can choose a life without death. Actually, however, to choose life is to choose death, since the temporal life we live as human beings terminates in death. To "accept" another form of life, one in which we shall never have to face death, is to accept an illusion. An earthly life without death is a mere dream. And even the acceptance of "eternal life" means for the Christian the prior acceptance of a temporal life that ends with death. Thus death cannot be evaded. It is a part of life, and it actually imparts meaning to life because it involves a basic contradiction that is essential for an understanding of human existence. Why should Christ have died on the cross if death were simply an absurdity? Christ's death rests on the presupposition that every death is tragic. And His death imparts to every death a dimension of hope and of victory. Christ on the cross hallowed the agony of love. The gift which Christ offers to those who love is the cross, and it is this gift which purifies love.

To love life as it really is means to accept it in its total reality, which includes death; to accept not only the *idea* of death but also those acts which anticipate death, in the offering and giving of ourselves.

As Unamuno told us, the materialistic definition of life as a "conjunction of functions which resist death" makes of life a struggle against truth; and "a struggle against death and thus also against truth, against the truth of death."

In a sense, every sacrifice of our personal interest and our pleasure for the sake of another person or simply for the act of "love" is a kind of death. But at the same time it is an act of life and an affirmation of the truth of life. Every time love accepts a partial "death," it reaffirms itself as life, triumphs over death and overcomes the self-contradiction of life within us. For this reason love actually demands this intrinsic contradiction to realize itself in our lives.

The metaphysical structure of love is in a certain sense dialectic. Love demands conflict; it nourishes itself by conflict and emerges purified from conflict. But once love attains to its authentic purity in the fire of conflict, it causes the conflict to disappear and with it disappears the contradiction. Thus, even in the midst of conflict, love is able to affirm with absolute certitude: "All things love each other; everything is love." And this is not merely an idea but rather the point of a concrete *act*. Without this act, the idea is meaningless.

Love, then, is both action and intuition. And, over and above these, it is a *presence*. It is an act by which our freely offered sacrifice transcends that contradiction of life and death which has its locus in the depth of our being. Love is an act of surrender and the intuition of a freedom beyond life and death, but of a freedom which can only be attained by self-surrender in the midst of self-contradiction. Love becomes perfect in a dialectic of action and intuition, culminating in the mysterious presence of Someone who is invisible but who *is love*. And now we understand that both the act and the intuition of love issue from this presence.

It is of such acts, such intuitions and such presences that these meditations were born, meditations which dare to affirm: there is nothing but love; everything is love. And all that which seems to be distinct from love and which even seems to contradict love, is in reality love. However, in order to see this, one has to love. One has to love wholly, totally, and one has to be willing to accept conflict and contradiction. One has to accept the death of love in order to be able to live the life of love. Once we accept this, we shall see that the conflict disappears and that in reality there is no contradiction, but only love.

A Master of Novices (at least this is my opinion) must above all be a man who does not meddle in affairs which are none of his business. A monastery is a *schola caritatis*—a school of love— but it is not men who are the teachers of love; it is the Spirit of Love that is the teacher of love. And it is the function of the human teacher to help the novice to listen to the authentic voice of the Spirit and not to allow himself to be deceived by forms of adulterated love, no matter how spiritual they may appear to be. This is why the monastery is an ideal school of freedom, in which the monk learns to obey in the incidentals of life in order to be free in what is essential, that is, free to love. And his love of God is a private personal problem for each individual. During the ten years that I was Master of Novices at Gethsemani Abbey in Kentucky, I never attempted to find out what the novices were writing down in the note-books they kept in their desks. If they wished to talk about it, they were free to do so. Ernesto Cardenal was a novice at Gethsemani for two years, and I knew about his notes and his poems. He spoke to me about his ideas and his meditations. I also knew about his simplicity, his loyalty to his vocation, and his dedication to love. But I never imagined that some day I was going to write an introduction to the simple meditations he was writing down in those days, nor that in reading them (almost ten years later) I would find in them so much clarity, profundity and maturity. What we meet here is more than a systematic doctrine: it is an intuitive knowledge of the profound truth of Christian life. A Christian is united with God in Christ through love. And so this book is entirely traditional—it reminds us at times of St. Augustine or of the mystics of "Bridal Union" of the German Rhineland—and yet entirely

17

modern, bearing resemblance to the vision of Teilhard de Chardin. And it is also absolutely sincere in its great simplicity, a quality which is surely one of the principal signs of the authenticity of spiritual teaching.

Ernesto Cardenal left Gethsemani because of ill health. However, today I can see that this is not the only reason: it did not make sense to continue at Gethsemani as a novice and as a student when actually he was already a teacher. Today he is an ordained priest and the founder of a contemplative community that lives in the spirit of the wisdom and in the humility of love which are so signally evident in these pages. His community is located precisely at a place where it is most needed—in Central America, where there are no contemplative religious orders. The book of Father Cardenal, this hymn to life and love, gives testimony of the renewal of the Church in Latin America. It is, we believe, a sign of the dawn of a new day in these countries of the future. They will not only attain temporal freedom and prosperity, but will also learn to sing hymns to life and to love, thus bringing to fruition the abundant potentialities that are still dormant and hidden in that rich, volcanic soil.

THOMAS MERTON

TO LIVE IS TO LOVE

ALL things love each other. All nature is oriental toward a *thou*. All beings that are alive are in communion with each other. All plants, all animals, all beings are fraternally united by the phenomenon of mimesis. There are insects which mimic flowers and flowers which act like insects, animals which resemble water or rocks or desert sand or snow or woodland or certain other animals. And thus all beings love each other or feed each other, and all are united in a gigantic process of birth and growth and reproduction and death. In nature everything undergoes mutation, transformation and change, everything embraces, caresses and kisses. And the laws which rule all animate beings and to which inert nature, too, obeys (for nature, too, is alive and animated by a life that is imperceptible to us) are variants of the one law of love. All physical phenomena are likewise manifestations of the identical phenomenon of love. The cohesion of a snowflake and the explosion of a "nova," the tumble-bug that clings to a heap of dung, and the lover who embraces his beloved, manifest the same phenomenon of love. Everything in nature seeks to transcend its own limitations, to go beyond the barriers of its individuality, to meet with a *thou* to which it can give itself, an "other" into which it can transform itself. The laws of thermodynamics and electrodynamics, the laws of the propulsion of light, and the universal law of gravity, are all manifestations of the one law of Love. Everything in nature is incomplete, and everything therefore is self-giving and embrace, and all beings are in their innermost essence and in the deepest mysterious ground of their existence hunger and thirst for love.

All things are related to each other, all are contained in one another, so that actually the universe forms one single colossal entity.

All nature is in close touch and interwoven. All nature is in constant embrace. The wind which caresses me and the sun which kisses me, the air which I inhale, and the fish which swims in the water, the distant star and I who behold it: we are all in closest touch with one another. What we call the empty interstellar spaces are molded by the same matter that informs the stars, even though in a tenuous and rarefied way. The stars are but condensed forms of interstellar matter, and the entire universe is like one single immense star; and we all participate in this universe in one and the same rhythm—the rhythm of that universal gravity which accounts for the cohesion of an otherwise chaotic matter, a cohesion which joins the molecules together and causes certain particles of matter to unite at a definite place of the universe and which makes the stars what they are. And this unifying force is the rhythm of love.

Though we are all in close contact, we are all incomplete. This incomplete nature of ours strives unceasingly for greater perfection, and this striving we call evolution. The most perfect being in nature is man. And yet man, too, is incomplete; he, too, is imperfect and he, too, tends toward a *Thou:* he tends toward God. And when man loves God, he loves Him with the same ardent desire that animates all nature; he loves Him with the groaning of all creatures, with the immense perennial desire of the entire process of evolution. All creation sighs with us, as St. Paul says, in the travails of birth, the travails of the tremendous process of evolution.

When the monks chant in choir, they chant in the name of all creation, because in every part and particle of nature, from the electron to man, we hear only one single psalm. And we cannot find rest until we find God. Then only will the great cosmic anguish in our heart be stilled; then only will that great love come to rest which weighs upon the small heart of man with the entire force of the universal law of gravity, until we encounter the Thou which is sought by all creatures.

And all things speak to us of God, because all things sigh for God: the starry sky no less than the crickets, the immense galaxies, the striped squirrel at play all the day long, fearing everything, hiding from everything (and ever moving unconsciously toward God).

Toward Him move all of the stars, all of the universe—toward Him from whom they have all come forth, and in Him only will they come to rest.

WHEN the lonely coyote howls in the night, he calls for You. And for You the night owl hoots. For You, not knowing it, sweetly coos the dove. And when the young calf calls for his mother, it calls for You, and the roaring lion cries for You, and the croaking of the frogs is meant for You. Thus all creation calls for You in multiple tongues. The language of rivers, of poets, of praying monks calls for You in its different idioms.

In the eyes of every human being there burns an insatiable desire. In the eyes of people of all races, in the looks of children and of old men, of mothers and of women in love, of policemen, of wage earners, adventurers, assassins, revolutionaries, dictators and saints there is the same spark of insatiable desire, the same hidden fire, the same bottomless abyss, the same infinite longing for happiness and joy and a never-ending possession of the ultimate end and aim of all striving. In all human eyes there is a deep well, the well of the Samaritan woman.

Every woman is this Samaritan woman at the well. And the well is very deep. And sitting on the curb-stone of the well is Jesus. "And the woman said to Him: 'Sir, you have nothing with which to draw the water, and the well is deep. . . .'"

And Jesus replied and said to her, "Whoever drinks of this water will get thirsty again; but he who drinks of the water that I shall give him will never be thirsty again, for the water that I shall give him will turn into a spring inside him and will well up to eternal life."

And the woman said to Him, "Sir, give me some of that water, so that I may never get thirsty again" (John 4, 11–15).

This thirst that is in all beings is the love of God.

It is because of that love that all crimes are committed, that all wars are fought, that all men love and hate one another. Because of this love people climb mountains and descend to the ocean floor. And because of this love people lord it over one another, conspire against one another, instruct and edify one another, write, sing, weep and love. Every human act, even sin, is a search for God. However, we often seek Him where he cannot be found. This is why St. Augustine wrote: "Go on seeking what you are after, but seek it elsewhere." For what one seeks in revelry, in festivities, in travels, in movies and bars, is nothing less than that God who can be found only in our interiority.

In the inner heart of all things the same fire is aglow, the same thirst burns: "As the hind thirsts for the current of water, so my soul thirsts for You, my God," sings the psalmist. Every heart is wounded by the same dart.

The insatiable desire of dictators, of kings of power, money and property, is the love of God. The lover who looks for the house of his beloved, the explorer, the businessman, the agitator, the artist, the contemplative recluse, are all in search of only one thing: heaven.

The faces of maidens are mirrors of heaven, and this is why they entrance us, since we were all created for heaven.

God is the fatherland of all men. God is our only homesickness. God calls to us from the innermost depth of all creatures, and He is the chant that echoes in all creatures. His call can be heard in our innermost being, like the sound of the lark that calls for its mate in the early dawn, like Romeo whispering his love to Juliet.

The evenings and the nights are quiet and deserted because God has made them for contemplation. The forests, the deserts, the sea and the starry sky have been made for contemplation. Indeed the entire world was made for contemplation. Magpies and fishes speak to us of God, and it is God who has taught them to speak. All the animals who sing at daybreak are singing for God. Volcanoes, clouds and trees speak to us of God with a loud voice. The entire creation proclaims resoundingly the existence, the beauty and the love of God. Music tells it to our ears and the scenic beauty of nature conveys the message to our eyes.

"I find letters from God dropt in the street, and everyone of them is signed by God's name," wrote Walt Whitman. A green leaf, in Whitman's words, is a fragrant handkerchief that bears God's initials in one corner, and He dropped it intentionally to remind us of Him. This is how the saints see nature, and this is how Adam saw it in Paradise (and poets and artists, like Adam and the saints, often look at nature in a similar way).

We find God's initials in all nature, and all creatures are God's messages of love addressed to us. They are flashes of His love. All nature is aflame with love, created by love in order to kindle love. This is the *raison d'être* of all beings and their one and only meaning. They can offer us no more perfect satisfaction and give us no greater pleasure than to kindle in us the love of God.

Nature is like the shadow of God, a reflection of His beauty and His splendor. The blue of the placid lake mirrors this divine splendor. God's fingerprints are impressed on every particle of matter. In every atom an image of the Trinity is enshrined, a faint resemblance of the Triune God. And this, Oh Lord, is why your creation fills us with rapturous enthusiasm.

My entire body, too, has been made to love God. Each of its cells is a hymn to the Creator and a continuous declaration of love. As the kingfisher has been made to catch fish and the hummingbird to suck flowers, so man has been made for the contemplation and love of God.

God is alive in every part and organ of man, not only in the soul. But He is deeply within the soul, too, and it is because man is aware of God's presence in the soul and because he wants to enjoy this presence that he withdraws into solitude and silence. He does not want any other creature's image in his soul except the image and reflection of God, just as the placid lake reflects only the sky.

God is mirrored in solitude and peace as heaven is mirrored in the placid lake. When the soul becomes pacified and purified, its surface begins to mirror the face of God. This face of God is the Son of Man, the same face that left its imprint on the veil of Veronica. It is a face that in a more opaque way makes its appearance in all of God's creation.

We are mirrors of God, created to return to Him. The water may still be turbid, but even in this condition it can reflect heaven.

ALL nature speaks with an articulate voice: everything in it is song, music and sound. All beings whisper, sigh, hum, quaver, chirp, roar, howl, bellow, groan, shriek, weep or murmur. The song of the crickets, the cicadas and the frogs, and the whistling with which the striped squirrels greet each other, and all the other voices of the fields are one great prayer. This is the reason for the silence observed by those contemplative monks who have dedicated their voices to the choral chant. They know that every voice is a prayer.

But everything in nature consists of symbols which speak of God. The whole of creation is pure caligraphy, and there is not a single stroke in it that is without meaning. The path of the meteors in the sky and the trail of the mollusks in the sand, the flight of the migratory birds in October nights, the circuit of the sun around the zodiac and the cycles of springs and winters engraved in the trunk of a cedar, the instantaneous contour traced by flashes of lightning and the serpentine course of rivers in aerial photographs, all are signs and signals transmitting a message to those who know how to read them. And those who enthusiastically contemplate the signs without deciphering them and without realizing that all nature was designed for them, are like a country girl who amuses herself by looking at the beautiful letters of a manuscript that has fallen into her hands, but who has never learned to read and who therefore does not know that these signs are a love letter which the emperor has written to her.

We, too, are a sign written by God, and we all bear inscribed within us the divine penmanship, and all our being is a communication and a message from God. As God's purest words we have been placed in the midst of this created world, which itself is nothing but a divine communication. We are images of God.

Man has made his gods in his own image and likeness because God has made man in His image and likeness.

The *raison d'être* of human love lies in the fact that the face of man is an image and likeness of the face of God. We love God in the faces of others. Every human face is covered with a veil, and the veil hides Him whom we cannot see face to face without dying.

We have been created by a *pluralistic* God, a God who in creating man used the grammatical plural ("Let Us make man in Our image and likeness"), and the image of this plurality, of God's Trinity, is reflected in every human being. The same may be said with regard to the image of love: because God is love (reciprocal love), we have been created in the image of a communitarian God.

The image of God that we bear within us is the Face of Christ. The Face of Christ is imprinted in our faces as it was imprinted in the veil of Veronica. The Face of Christ is imprinted in everything that is beautiful, in the face of every woman. St. John Climacus tells of a man who was seized by a burning love of God whenever he saw a beautiful woman; shedding tears, he gave glory to God.

To the Jewish people it was forbidden to make images of God, because man (Christ) is Himself the image of God. And even animals are in their own way images of God because they are images of man, who is the image of God (and this is why man loves the animals).

The image of God has been dimmed by sin (the demons have

faces in which the image of God has been blotted out), but with the coming of Christ, God's image has been restored in man. In Christ we are again image and word of God, for He is the Logos, the Word and the Image of the Father ("he who sees me, sees my Father").

The Word of God (the Logos) is a word that reveals itself to us only in silence.

This divine Word speaks in the depth of every being, and it speaks within our own selves. To find it we do not have to travel far, we do not have to go out of ourselves. And we do not have to travel far to find happiness; it suffices to descend into the depth of our own being to discover our true identity (that is, God). However, modern man always tries to flee from himself. He can never be silent or alone, because that would mean to be alone with himself, and this is why the places of amusement and the cinemas are always filled with people. And when they find themselves alone and are at a point where they might encounter God, they turn on the radio or the television set.

PRAYER is as natural to man as speaking, sighing and seeing, as natural as the palpitation of a loving heart; and actually that is what prayer is: a murmur, a sigh, a glance, a heartbeat of love. It is something natural to man, a natural instinct, but man in his fallen nature has to learn it anew, because it is a forgotten instinct.

Prayer is nothing more than getting into intimate contact with God. It is communication with God, and as such it need not be expressed in words, nor even articulated mentally. One can communicate with a glance of the eye, with a smile, with a sigh, as well as by a human act. Even smoking can be a prayer, or the painting of a picture, or a look toward heaven or the taking of a drink of water. All our bodily acts are of the nature of prayer. Our body performs a perfect physiological act of thanksgiving when, thirsting, it receives into itself a glass of water. Or, when on a hot day we bathe in a cool river, our skin sings a hymn of thanksgiving in praise of the Creator, even though this kind of prayer may be non-rational, unconscious and at times involuntary. However, we are able to transform everything we do into prayer. Work and labor are forms of existential prayer. Our Lord told Angela de Foligno that He was taking pleasure in everything she was doing, whether she was eating, drinking or sleeping; that He was taking pleasure in her entire being and in the exercise of all her organic functions.

In the *Fioretti* we are told about the prayer of Brother Maseo that it consisted in repeating the vowel "U, U, U, U"; and the prayer of Brother Bernardo consisted in running around a mountain.

God surrounds us on all sides like the air. And like the atmosphere he emits visible and audible waves, and we are unable to see and hear them unless we are tuning in on the proper channels. Thus the divine waves are all around us, but we are unable to identify them as coming from Him unless we are in tune with them. Those who live only in the world of sense perception are unable to receive these waves of God.

We are able to communicate with one another by way of God, not unlike a tele-communication by way of the atmosphere. Thus two friends or two lovers are able to communicate with each other through space, even though they may live in far distant cities. Even in such great distance they can be more united than two neighbors who live wall to wall in a small village.

However, God is also infinitely far from us. We are separated from Him by an infinite difference. And any union with God resembles always that of two lovers who are separated by a wall of glass, and even their kisses are separated in this manner.

We see God in a dark light. We may compare the way we see Him with what happens with a picture on a screen: it cannot be seen clearly until the doors are closed and the lights extinguished, and the darker the room becomes, the clearer are the forms and figures of the picture. Or we may compare the way we see God with what happens in a house in which all lights have been turned off except one brightly shining lamp in one room of the interior; we are groping insecurely in the dark, tripping over pieces of furniture, wandering through flights of rooms and hallways, but guided by the hand of someone who is familiar with the outlay of the mansion.

The presence of God remains opaque and veiled, and it becomes more indistinct the nearer we approach Him. It is as if a transparent, delicate film were interposing itself between our perception and the perceived reality. And we must never try to break through this opaqueness to tear apart the veil. The fact is that we are so close to Him that we are unable to see Him.

The reason why men ordinarily do not experience the presence of God lies in the fact that all of our everyday experiences come to us from the outside, whereas this experience comes from within. We are oriented toward the external, depending on external sensations, and here all of a sudden we are being touched and addressed from within.

We even labor under the illusion that if God were to speak to us He would speak with a material voice, that he would enter into us by way of our ears.

Or we may believe that we ourselves are this divine presence, and we may therefore remain unaware of His presence within us. We do not know that in the interior of our being we are not ourselves but belong to an Other. That our true identity is this Other; that thus each one of us is, ontologically speaking, not one single entity, but *two;* that to encounter ourselves and anchor ourselves in our innermost being is to fling ourselves into the arms of that Other.

We are forever in search of that embrace, but this search is ambiguous in that it is oriented toward the external. We can hear the irresistible voice of the Beloved calling from within, but we believe that the call comes from outside.

Let us never forget that God is everywhere, even on Broadway, but we can hear His voice only in the silence of our interiority.

For Santa Teresa of Avila life is like a night we have spent in a poor village inn, and for Cervantes, too, human dream-castles resemble such poor inns. However, for Santa Teresa the soul itself is a castle that resembles the castles of the Castilian high plateaus. And our interiority, the center of our being, wherein God dwells, is the bridal chamber of this castle. But for most men this interior chamber is a dark prison cell to which they never descend. And yet there is indeed such a secret and hidden dwelling place, such a bridal chamber, in each of us.

Deeply within ourselves resides love. God is superabundance of love, and therefore His behavior is unpredictable. At any moment the divine Lover may do something very extravagant, for, like any lover, He does not reason. He is drunk with love.

The soul resembles a secret room to which only God has the key, and unless He enters, the room will be vacant. The senses may satiate themselves with pleasures ad nauseam, but the soul will remain empty.

I have seen Venice and Capri and was fascinated by their beauty, but I was not satisfied. Something was missing. In the underground of every joy there lurks a certain melancholy and an inner anguish. And today my memories are less real than picture postcards. It all seems no more than a deceptive mirage.

Every beauty carries with it an element of sadness. Deeply within all things there hides some bitterness and a sigh of pain. This is that cosmic sigh or groan of which St. Paul speaks.

However, in man the created world is liberated from this metaphysical agony when the human heart finds rest in God.

One gets easily tired of motion pictures, of festivities, of yachting, but one gets never tired of God. Trappist monks have no need of periods of recreation, because their entire life is recreation. Neither have birds and squirrels need of recreation, because their entire life, too, even when they labor in search of food, is recreation and perpetual play.

How much would the barons of oil and steel pay to buy this kind of peace? They might be willing to give their empires of oil and steel in exchange for the knowledge and experience of this peace, just as all of those who have acquired this knowledge and experience have paid for it with all of their possessions. For what the millionaires seek in money is happiness, and any one of them would give all of his material fortune if he knew that happiness can be found elsewhere (the members of religious orders have given all they possessed, or could have possessed, in search for this kind of happiness).

How many young people are perhaps at this hour at festivals, in cinemas, in bars and nightclubs, while actually God has called them to the mystical life! He has perhaps reserved for them the highest gifts of contemplation, but they do not know it and will perhaps never know it in this life.

How many are there who are clinging to the pleasures of sense with a mystical fervor? They seek God where He cannot be found, and the fact that they do not find Him may drive them to despair, to vice, to crime, to insanity and suicide. They are seeking happiness in money, in women, in drink, in nightclubs, and they may do so with all those splendid faculties which were made for the Beatific Vision.

A young girl whose heart is filled with dreams of love and a longing for tender affection, a girl who is most loving or most desirous of love, most desirous of life and of romance, is also the one who is most capable of surrendering her entire self to Jesus. He is the one whom she really seeks in her dreams, in her attendance at dances, but, alas, she does not find Him.

We have been created for love, for a God who is Love, and the most intense and profound suffering of the human being as well as the most intense pain of each of us are caused by love. How many of us will have a monotonous and barren worldly life, a life without love, always longing for a love which might bring us fulfillment but which never arrives! And there are many others who experience the bitterness of a despairing or unrequited love or the torments of wasted, forbidden love, none of whom can ever find fulfillment. Others experience the sadness of satisfied love but yet without fulfillment. And yet how capable would all these be of fulfilled love, how fully could they satisfy their almost limitless capacity for love, for tenderness and for surrender to another person if only they would turn inward to their own selves, to that unsatiated love which in their own interiority breathes and throbs! These poor lives could so easily be transformed into continuous rapture, into a lasting idyl, into perpetual joy and ecstasy, into a veritable paradise of love. However, these poor lives are without love: they have nothing but the sensation of the passage of time, the passage of spring, the process of aging, and love never arrives. They may well live to see another spring, but they will never experience the advent of love.

GOD is love. And man, too, is love, because man was made in God's image and likeness.

God is love. And since He is an infinitely simple Being, if He is love, He can be nothing more and nothing less than love. When we say that He is the infinite Good, infinite Wisdom, infinite Truth, infinite Beauty and infinite Justice, we do not mean that He is a Love that is infinitely good, infinitely wise, infinitely true, infinitely beautiful and infinitely just. We rather mean that He is nothing but Love.

And man, made in the image of God, is likewise nothing but love. When man awakens to his rational life, he becomes aware of the fact that his entire being is one single desire, one single passion, one single thirst and shout of love.

The unadulterated substance of our being is love. Ontologically we are love. And God, like ourselves, is likewise a single call and shout of love, an infinite passion, an infinite thirst for love. This love is the reason of our existence.

And this love of God and our own love are one and the same love, a love which we can never extinguish. In this it resembles the fires of hell or a thirst that can never be stilled, because the more we try to satisfy it, the more insatiable it becomes.

We retain in our being and in all our motions a remembrance of God from whom we have come, even though we may be far from Him, not unlike those creatures of the sea which even in the aquarium cannot forget the open sea and move day in and day out in accord with the rhythm of the ocean waves, no matter how far they may be removed from their natural habitat.

The heart of the Father, too, cannot be at rest until the entire creation, like the Prodigal Son, returns to His bosom. We are the objects of an infinite nostalgic longing on the part of the Father, and the Holy Spirit is the sigh of this nostalgia.

The Word of God has become incarnate in us by our love of self and by our love of the Father, in such a way that we can love the Father in ourselves and that God can love His own Self in millions of souls and in millions of lives.

We are an invention of Love, and we were created to love. We are the conductor wires for the high tension current of love, and this is why there is no room in us for selfish love, because every selfish love acts as an insulator. Therefore we must love our fellow men as we love ourselves, since to love ourselves more than we love them would impede and inhibit our love. We must give ourselves wholly to love and allow its current to flow through us; we are transmitters of love.

Every created being, by the mere fact of its existence, is in communion with the Being of God, but in irrational beings this communion is limited and imperfect. Man is the only creature in the universe who is capable of loving God with his whole conscious being. Every man is born with a wounded heart that resembles the pierced heart of Jesus. And man is surely not a meaningless passion, as Jean-Paul Sartre claims, but a passion the meaning of which is God.

38

SANCTITY expresses our true personality. Just as no two leaves are alike, so also no two human beings are alike. Sin, however, makes equals of us all; it makes us look like prisoners wearing the same uniform. Contrariwise, every saint is different, because sanctity is the full realization of the human personality, a recovery of that aboriginal identity which all beings once had and which they have lost by sin.

The more we become identical with God, the more we become truly ourselves. Our greater identification with God is the mark of our greater personal identity. We may mistakenly believe that we are God by our essence but—and this is saying almost, but not quite, the same thing—in our essence we are images of God.

And thus, the more the soul resembles God, the more it is itself, because it is destined to be a portrait—a self-portrait—of God. The soul is not infinite, but it is an image of the infinite, and this again is saying almost, but not quite, the same thing.

We do not know what the beauty of the soul is like because we have not seen its beauty. But what we have seen is the absence of soul in the ugliness of a body from which the soul has departed. The frozen grin of a cadaver can, by contrast, give us an idea of what the soul is like. And, in turn, the beauty of a be-souled body can give us an idea of what the beauty of a naked soul must be like. This idea can also be conveyed by great works of art, in which we see mirrored the soul of the artist. It can be equally well conveyed when we discover the mystery of the soul in the intimacy of friendship or of love.

The love and the beauty of God impart beauty to the soul; and a soul that mirrors God is a soul aflame with the fire of love. In such a soul an infinite beauty and an infinite love are reflected, as the deep blue of heaven is mirrored in the Lake of Nicaragua in the month of May.

The naked soul is all smiles, all feeling and love, all pulsation, fervor, passion and flame, all tenderness and sensitivity, vitality and life. And the more the soul is united with God in contemplation, the better it gets to know Him; and the better it knows Him, the more it loves Him; and the more it loves Him, the more it gains a hold of Him. Thus the Soul's knowledge and love of God increase continuously, and its entire life consists in giving and receiving, in ever increasing vibrant joy and pulsating love.

Before God, the soul is womanly, passive and purely receptive. It does not take the initiative. The soul cannot come to God as a visitor, for it does not know the way and the place where He abides. It rather lives in the hope that He may pay a visit, and if He does not come, the soul will remain alone. The soul is unable to initiate the move toward God. It is God rather who enters and leaves, who visits and departs. Nor does the soul know how to embrace God caressingly, and only very shyly does it dare at times to show its deep affection. But it knows very well how to let Him caress it, and actually this is the only thing it knows how to do well. The soul does not know how to kiss its Beloved, but it is He who kisses the soul with great tenderness and at times even passionately. And thus the soul allows itself to be kissed and is aflame with love.

The soul of an old woman is as young and fresh as the soul

40

of a child or a young girl, for the soul is a fountain of vitality and does not age with the passage of time, and the soul of the coarsest man is as overflowing with light as the soul of a Beethoven or a Dante, and the soul of a man is as feminine as the soul of a woman. The soul is the root principle of life, and it is wholly innocent, pure light, joyfulness, lucidity, sweetness and grace, and this is why God is madly in love with the soul. And every man whom you see walking in the street has this kind of a soul. It is therefore all the sadder that such a soul may allow itself to be embraced by far inferior lovers, that it may allow itself to be enslaved by food and drink, by all kinds of diversions and, last but not least, by money.

Sometimes we get a small glimpse of the beauty of the soul in the purity of human eyes, in eyes in which some of the splendor of the soul is filtered through the density of matter as sunlight is filtered through eyelids that are closed.

As long as the body is alive, soul and body are one, and the soul in this case is no more than the corporeal reality and vitality, that is to say, the principle which makes the body differ from a cadaver. "And if the body were not the soul, what is the soul?" asks Walt Whitman. This was stated much earlier by Aristotle when he said that the soul is the substance which in-forms (or gives form to) the body.

The reflection of God in the opaqueness of matter dazzles us, and this reflection is that splendor which is a property of all beautiful things. But how dazzling must then be the beauty of God when it is reflected not in opaque matter but in a pure godlike spirit. The essence of the many beauties of nature, that common denominator which is present in everything beautiful (in the blue sea, in lakes, in snow-covered mountains, in deserts, in women, flowers and stars), is likewise present in such a soul,

41

but in concentrated form, developed, refined, transformed into a higher kind of beauty, which in its pure spirituality resembles the spirit of God. It is like a concentration of thousands of smiles or a concentration of many landscapes, so as to form a coherent whole, and it is even much more than that.

"My daughters," said Santa Teresa, "we are not hollow inside."

GOD loves us not *en masse* but individually. The mere fact of being is proof of His infinite and eternal love, because from all eternity He has chosen us out of an infinite number of possible beings, from whom He has set us apart, thus decreeing for them non-existence. And among all the beings of His choice He has chosen each of us in particular. Only we were called into being, and not out of thousands or millions of beings, but out of an infinitude of beings whom He might have chosen in our place, and yet He did not create them. Thus we are His choice among an infinitude of possibilities, and the mere fact that we exist proves God's preferential love for us.

Each and every one of us is irreplaceable, like a unique masterpiece in a collection, for God is an artist who never repeats or copies Himself. Neither a leaf nor a person's fingerprints are ever the same, and this is true also of the soul: it is always unique. And a soul that is lost is never duplicated in all eternity, and God feels this loss eternally.

God loves each and every one of us more than we love ourselves. He loves us as only God can love, and He loves us as He loves Himself, and how much pain must it cause Him to find Himself eternally separated from any one of us.

God is love. But He is often unrequited love, and this is a great tragedy for God. We often conceive of Him as a tyrant who demands more and ever more of us, but in reality He is always entreating love. Imagine, the Creator of the universe begging for your love!

GOD loves each and every individual person as though there existed only two beings in the entire cosmos: God and this individual. God does not need man in order to be happy, but He loves man as though He would be eternally unhappy without man. Although He has lived from all eternity without being in need of man, He humiliates Himself like a slave out of love for us, as though He were unable to live for even one single moment without us. God so much loves the soul, said St. Catherine of Genoa, that it might appear as if God were a slave and the soul were God.

Sometimes God seems to have forgotten the entire universe as though his only desire were to converse with us.

Like a lover who thinks unceasingly of his distant beloved, so You, my God, have dreamed of me since long before I was born, dreamed of me from all eternity.

We in our turn are a homesickness for God, that great nostalgia which each of us bears within himself at the time of his birth. To be, for us, is to live in exile, far away from God. God is love, and we, too, who were created in God's image, are love. All of our cells are love, created for love, as the grain of incense is created for fire, and all our being consists of the embers of this fire.

The only thing that separates us from God is our ego, our self-love. This is why union with God can come about only by

44

the death of the ego. It is either God or I, and as soon as the ego passes out of sight, God begins to dwell in us.

When we learn to repeat the *Fiat* of Mary, God becomes incarnate in us also. The transubstantiation which then takes place in us resembles the transubstantiation of water and wine, for then our own flesh and blood are being transformed into Christ, into the body and blood of God. We ourselves then become a eucharist, a holocaust of love.

For St. Bernard the mystical union is a mutual consuming one of the other, of God and the soul. Love always tends to make two things into one. But here on earth two beings can never become wholly one. God succeeds in achieving total unity with the soul only when both cease being two.

God is love. And is there any greater happiness than to love and to be loved? God is happiness because He is love and because He is this happiness of love. He is the infinite happiness of infinite love.

All that exists has sprung from God's love. All things were made by love, and all things are love.

God would not have created a single thing had He hated it, as we read in the Book of Wisdom (11, 24-25), and the mere fact that God sustains it is proof that He loves it. Thus the very existence of all things testifies to the fact that God loves them; their existence is due to God's kiss and embrace.

Picasso spoke well when he said "we do not know what a tree or a window really is." All things are very strange and mysterious (like some of Picasso's paintings), and if we forget about their strange and mysterious character, it is because we are so used to seeing them. Actually we have only a dim knowledge of the nature of things. What, after all, *are* things? They are God's love turned into things.

God communicates with us by way of all things. They are messages and messengers of His love. When I am reading a book, it is He who speaks to me through its pages. I raise my eyes to look at a landscape, and I realize that it is God who has created this landscape, so that I should see it. And it was God who has inspired the artist to paint the picture at which I looked today, so that I should see it. Everything that gives me joy was lovingly given by God so that I might enjoy it, and every pain, too, is God's loving gift.

God's love has created the world and keeps on creating it at every moment of the process of evolution. For God, the Creator, is also God the Sustainer of the evolving universe, and this evolution is the work of His love. When He said, "Grow and multiply," He laid down the Law of Evolution.

The world is not like a painting which an artist painted some centuries ago and which hangs now on the wall of some museum. The world rather resembles a work of art that is in a continuous process of creation in the workshop of the artist.

God is not made of marble, Paul told the Athenians gathered at the Areopagus in Athens, surrounded by their marble statues. God is no statue but rather the Living God in whom "we live and move and have our being." From Him derive the marble sculptures of the Areopagus as well as the hand which formed the marble and the inspiration that moved this hand.

Each of us believes that he is the center of the universe, and this is why we live in a fictitious universe, not unlike the astronomers who preceded Copernicus. We take interest only in things which serve our small personal concerns. But we can achieve happiness only when we realize that God is the center of our universe. Then only will we begin to enjoy everything that exists, and we will be glad that things are the way they are and that everything happens the way it does, because this is what God wants, regardless of whether or not it serves our little personal interests.

God is love, but our own love is self-love and therefore the very opposite of God's love, for true love is the self-giving of one person to another, while self-love is self-retention or the refusal of personal self-giving. Self-love is love in reverse. It is a love that has turned in on one's own self and thus actually does not differ from hate of others.

To love others as we love ourselves is a precept that is difficult to put into practice and even difficult to conceive of. What it describes is the natural condition of man when he lived in Paradise, for the paradisiacal state *is* man's aboriginal natural condition. Man, though created as an organic whole, is a composite of individualities: "Thus God created man in His own image; in the image of God He created him, and He created them male and female" (Gen. 1, 27). Thus we are one body, composed of innumerable individualities, and individual egotism is as antinatural as is the egotism of a cell of our individual organism which, self-centered, gives preference to its own selfish interest as opposed to the organic functioning of the whole, thus waging war against all the other cells. This condition we know as cancer. And self-love is the cancer of the Mystical or Cosmic Body. In St. Paul's words, "The eye cannot say to the hand, 'I do not need you,' nor can the hand say to the feet, 'I do not need you'" (1 Cor. 12, 21).

ALL nature is *charity*, but only the mystic experientially lives this kind of love. God's love surrounds us on all sides. His love is the water we drink and the air we breathe and the light we behold. All natural phenomena are but different forms of God's love. We move in His love as the fish swims in the water. We are so close to Him, so saturated with His love and with His gifts (even we ourselves are one of His gifts), that we fail to recognize it, because we lack perspective. His love surrounds us on all sides, but we fail to notice it, as we fail to notice the pressure of the atmosphere.

Nature is the love of God identifiable in sense perception, in materialized form. His providence becomes visible in everything we behold. Men hurry in the streets, busy with their many preoccupations and cares, without stopping for a moment to think of Him and to remember that it is in Him that they move, that He surrounds them on all sides and that all the hairs of their heads "are counted," as are all the cells of their bodies. Why then all our cares and preoccupations?

Why do men walk through their cities with their faces preoccupied, as if each one of them were alone in a strange and hostile universe in which he had to struggle unaided? Why do we worry about what to eat and drink, how to clothe ourselves and what merchandise to buy? Look at the birds in the sky and the lilies in the fields. Look at the sea anemone, at the humble protozoön and at the Omega Centaurus: they all do neither sow nor reap; they do not have warehouses or bank accounts or life insurance policies!

God's providence has lovingly taken care of the earth for billions of years, and He has watched over birds and insects for many millions of years, but you think you are helpless and alone in the universe, and you walk preoccupied with your daily chores as though no one cared for you. You forget that Someone at every moment takes care of every sinew of your body, controls the circulation of your blood and the functioning of all your glands. And you seem convinced that some small problem of your daily life can be solved by no one in the universe but yourself!

He hears the cry of the deer in the glade, calling for his mate. And He answers his call. He takes care of the cuckoo who asks for food. He guides the cranes on their flight. When the weasel and the badger are asleep in their burrows, He watches over them. The frog, the beetle and the raven are finding their nourishment every day at the right hour.

> All eyes look for you, Oh Lord,
> You feed all your creatures throughout the year.
> You open your hand and shower blessings on all
>   living beings.

(Psalm 104)

EVERY human being is born inwardly wounded by God's love, born with a thirst:

> Like thirsting ground my soul yearns for You.
> (Psalm 142)

The Creator has given nature food and drink as material symbols of His love.

This thirst for God is the cause of the anxiety we see in the faces of all the people walking in the streets, in the faces of those who are visiting the shops, the cinemas and the bars. All the world is driven onward by a desire, by many desires, by an infinity of desires: one more drink, one more piece of candy, one more gaze, one more word, one more kiss, one more trip. Always this craving for more and more and more. All faces are wounded by anxiety and desire. And those who have escaped from this enslavement by desires feel like those men and women who have escaped from the Nazi concentration camps and the forced labor camps of Siberia. Even though one may believe that one could well do with just a little more, one always seems to end up by desiring more and more. One may believe that one could do well with a small house and a car, a beautiful wife and children, but man always seems to go on walking with the same anxiety in his face. He goes on looking for new things with the same greed. He buys the newspaper with the same eagerness and then tosses it into the street and remains as dissatisfied as ever. It is like a sickness that compels us to stuff and gorge ourselves with food and drink without ever being satiated.

As Plato said, the human body is like a broken jug that can never be filled. The senses may be filled to overflowing with pleasures, but the soul remains hungry and thirsty, because these peripheral sensual pleasures have not penetrated to the soul and have served only, as it were, to irritate the mouth and make it water, because it feels that the cup of the longed-for happiness has not reached the lips.

It is as though we were trying to live on food that does not nourish or to feast on wine that does not inebriate. Food fills us and wine may make us drunk, but they do not satisfy our inmost desire but rather intensify it, so that actually they neither truly nourish nor inebriate. They may cause disgust, but they never satiate us.

As we may get an idea of the depth of a well by throwing a stone into it and do not hear it strike bottom, so we get an idea of the depth of our soul when things enter and disappear into it without our hearing them fall to the ground.

Since God is in the deepest ground of each soul, this ground is unfathomable, and it can be filled only by God. A wine which satisfies completely would have to have qualities of the infinite, not unlike that water which Christ offered the Samaritan woman at the well. It is such a wine.

Yet in cloisters one can see human beings walking who are satisfied and fulfilled, men and women who smile, who show in their faces none of the wrinkles of anxiety. St. Ignatius of Loyola once said that if he were ordered to dissolve his Society of Jesus, he would regain the same inner peace within fifteen minutes.

And so it is in the case of animals, too. They never run around in anxiety but walk about tranquil and fulfilled like monks and nuns.

Human beings are never satisfied with the things of this earth because they were not created for these things. Animals satisfy their needs, and that is all they desire. There is in them no thirst for the infinite, and so this earth is their heaven. This is why animals are never disappointed with life and never commit suicide; they were created for this earth. And all animals in their saintly animality are, in a manner of speaking, saints: they are chaste and poor and obedient and humble like monks.

All our own being, however, was designed for the love of God, designed to possess Him and to be happy in this possession, as the body of the mackerel was designed to swim in the water and the body of the sea-gull to fly over the sea.

As a telephone is designed to speak through and for no other function, so man was created to be happy in the possession of God and for no other ultimate end. And thus we are truly happy only with and in God.

Although we have never seen God, we are very much like migratory birds or fishes, who were born in a strange place, but when winter comes they feel a mysterious restlessness, a call in their blood, a homesickness for a primeval fatherland, a land they have never seen, and they depart for it without knowing whither they go. They have heard the call of the Promised Land. They have heard the voice of the Beloved who calls:

> Come then, my love,
> My lovely one, come!
> And see, winter is past,
> The rains are over and gone.
> (Song of Songs 2, 10)

THE soul is born in love, but it does not see the One who is the object of its love. However, since this lover is mirrored in all created things, the soul is born with a desire to embrace all things. The baby reaches out with its little arms for everything it sees; it tries to take into its mouth everything it touches, and it wants to touch and swallow everything. Later, when the child grows up, he wants to hug and grasp his toys, and when the child has finally become a mature person, the desire to embrace all things is no less potent. However, this desire is never fully actualized and satisfied, because what man embraces is not God, unless it happens that one day he detaches himself from things and actually does embrace God.

God, however, can be encountered only in nothingness, for God is found only where things have vanished. Things can never be fully possessed, and this is why they leave us always with an unstilled hunger.

"Oh world, never to be able to embrace you wholly!", exclaims Edna Saint Vincent Millay, the poetess who celebrated in song so many embraces. And this is the great anguish of the human heart: the desire to possess the world and not to be able to fulfill this desire (we remember Alexander who wept because he was unable to conquer the stars). And in love we desire to possess a human body, but here, too, the body of the beloved can never be wholly possessed. Only God can be totally possessed. Only God can be truly embraced, because the arms of the human soul were created for the infinite, for nothing more and nothing less.

Thus neither the world nor the woman we love can be truly and wholly embraced or possessed, and neither the world nor a woman can fully satisfy human desire, for only God can do that.

God gives us the happiness of perfect contentment and a drunkenness which does not depend on the consumption of wine. He is Himself that raptured inebriation. He is the sum total of all pleasures, joys and delights and of all love. He is all that in infinite measure and thus quite unlike the shadows of pleasures, joys and delights and the shadows of love which we have chased after.

In Him is con-centered the beauty of all women, the savor of all fruits, the inebriation produced by all wines and the sweetness and bitterness of all earthly loves; to taste one drop of God is to remain in ecstatic rapture forever.

A human being who has tasted one drop of this bliss can no longer live as before; he cannot attend to his daily routine at the office and pursue his social conventions, for he is like a madman who may commit all kinds of follies. He may run out into the street clad only in rags or with a paper bag on his head, causing people to make fun of him, or he may preach at street corners, or he may lock himself up in a cell for the rest of his days, or he may kiss the lepers. He embodies what people mean when they speak of "conversion."

To love God has now become my only reason for my existence, my one and only profession, vocation and occupation. I have surrendered myself to You, my God, with the same passion with which in former years I gave myself to the beauty of young women, and I have now given myself wholly to You as formerly I gave myself wholeheartedly to them. And I know that I will

55

find in You the familiar features of all those beautiful faces that I have loved in the course of my life. I love You with the same love which I formerly felt for all the things that are formed by Your hands and particularly with the love which I felt for young maidens, the most beautiful among your creations, whom in my earlier life I loved with the impetuosity and the intensity of my love of God, and whom now I love no longer. Love has remained, but the former objects of my love have disappeared. The thirst has remained, the burning heat of the Sahara Desert, a hunger for love of almost cosmic proportions, an insatiable anxiety, a heart that had to be emptied to be filled by You. All my former loves have died, and Your love only remains, that love for You whom now I love with all the love I have. Have mercy, Lord, on my poor and empty heart.

GOD is love. However, every love is love of something or of someone. Whom, then, does God love? He loves God, of course. Love loves love. And this love for love in its turn is again love for love, and so on ad infinitum, and this is why God is infinite. He is infinite love for an infinite love or, to put it differently, He is an infinite commerce or interchange of love.

God is commutuality. He is simultaneously one and two, two united in one, and this commutual union of two in one is again God, and thus God is also one and three. Love for love means that God is a Love that loves itself, not unlike a mirror that is mirrored in another mirror, so that there is an infinite number of mirrors or one mirror with an infinite number of reflections.

God is Tri-Une because He is Love and thus an infinite projection, procreation and transmission of Himself and a never ending outpouring of love. He is One because He is love, unity, self-identity and a communion of lover and beloved in the embrace of love.

To love God is to partake of Him, because God is this kind of self-love. However, God's love is not a selfish love but a love that is self-giving, for God is not an egotistic self-love but a commutual self-love.

To love others is likewise a partaking of God, for that which we love in others is the divine spark in them. And it is the divine spark in us which causes us to love others. And what the others love in us is that which is god-like in us. All commutual love, therefore, bears some resemblance to that God who loves Himself commutually.

Those who love one another, communicate to each other a gift that is the very substance of God. If God were only unity, He would be totally alone, without progeny, and He would therefore be a God without love, a sterile God. However, He is unity and diversity at one and the same time. And all diversity and the innumerable divers things in creation proceed from Him, as does all individuality and unity in things. Our union with one another is an image of the divine Union. And union of us all with and in Christ is a participation in the Union of the Trinity.

God's self-love is not a selfish love but rather the love of one Person for another Person, for an infinite Other. There is an infinite difference between these two Persons, and their mutual love becomes manifest in yet another infinite Person who also is God.

If and as long as we are free from selfishness, the Son loves His Father in and through us as through a conductor wire, with a kind of love which is God also: this we call the Holy Spirit, "the Spirit of Our Lord Jesus Christ," in the words of St. Paul.

The Holy Spirit is thus the love of the two divine Persons, its spiration, its breath and its kiss. The Word is the word of God, and the Holy Spirit is the sigh of God, a lullaby of love. The Son is a projection and manifestation of God in the form of a divine dialogue, and the Holy Spirit is the sigh of two lovers.

What we call the dogma of love, the dogma of the Holy Trinity, is the revelation of the mystery that God is not alone, that God is union, Communion and Commun-ism.

St. Ignatius of Loyola was moved to tears whenever he saw on his walks through the streets of Rome things that were three in number: three doves, three men, three stars in the heavens, three children at play, because all these reminded him of the mystery of Trinitarian love. The Trinity is love. And every human family, consisting of father, mother and child, is an image of the Trinity. So is the fertility of nature, for in nature, too, everything is Trinitarian: all existing things are the off-spring of other things, and every particular thing is united with another, and of their union proceeds something new.

God is Three and One, but His Plurality differs from our metrical system in which we count from one to four. God's Plurality is an infinite One and an infinite Three, and therein is contained every plurality and every unity.

God is above all numbers, as His name (the Word) is above every name, for while every other word and every other number signifies and symbolizes a specific thing, the Infinite Word is the very thing it signifies, namely, infinitude. The Infinite Word is an infinite name of an infinite reality, and the name *is* that very reality. When God revealed His name, He said, "I Am Who Am," that is, I am He whose existence is comprised in His name. He is the One whose only name is To Be. His name is Existence. And this is the name by which the Father called His Son: "a name that is above every name," as we read in St. Paul. This means that the Divine Name transcends all seman-tics and all human language. Your "glorious and terrible name, oh God, is Y.A.H.W.E.H." (Deuteronomy 28, 58).

THE atheist who denies the existence of God, affirms a partial truth, namely, God's non-existence or the fact that God's existence is unlike that of everything else. Theologians call this God's "transcendence." And Dionysius the Areopagite, Meister Eckart, Henry Suso and other mystics call God the Naught, the Great No-Thing. For God is no thing like all other things but, compared with them, He is indeed No-Thing or the Naught. He thus is Non-being. And since we predicate "existence" of things, we are forced to the conclusion that God does not exist. On the other hand, if we predicate "existence" of God, then nothing else "exists." To say it quite simply: God differs so much from everything that exists that it would seem that He does not exist. But if He exists, then everything else is as nothing before Him. In a certain sense, then, God does not exist, and again in a certain sense He alone exists.

In a certain sense the atheists are also correct when they deny God if God is conceived of anthropomorphically. An anthropomorphic God does indeed not exist, but is no more than a childish fiction. But if they are convinced that some vaguely conceived, incomprehensible entity does exist, some mysterious, unknown and nameless Being which they refuse to call God but endow with divine attributes, then they actually, even though obscurely, affirm the existence of God, that is, of a Being that can not be comprehended nor even imagined and that no one can see face to face without dying. Their God is then the Unknown God of whom St. Paul spoke to the Athenians on the Areopagus when he told them that their Unknown God was indeed the True God and that they were worshipping Him without knowing it.

God is not only light but also darkness. And the idea of the "Naught" which the atheists have of God is identical with the kind of knowledge the mystics claim to have gained *experientially ("cognitio experimentalis Dei")*: they have personally experienced this Naught and have affirmed that it is an unfathomable abyss of sweetness and love, and they have felt its tender embrace.

God is simultaneously light and darkness or, to put it differently, He is neither light nor darkness, but when He created the world, He separated for us light from darkness and made us "children of Light." We do not possess the full knowledge of good and evil but only the knowledge of good, for we were created for the good, and we were created in light, jointly with everything that exists. The full knowledge of good and evil is the exclusive privilege of God. And the mystical experience is an experience of God's darkness or of that divine reality in which there is not that separation of light from darkness which for us is the distinguishing mark of night and day. For God is also the Creator of the night, and He is Night, too: the night of love and the night of mystery. And we, who have come from this Night, bear within ourselves a nostalgic longing for the darkness of the night.

God is infinitely beautiful, but we might also say that there is in Him not only beauty but also a certain "ugliness," because His "beauty" is wholly different from our aesthetic canons. "In order to create something new one must always make it look ugly," wrote Picasso. And God is an infinite Novelty. And, as St. Paul said, we know the invisible perfection of God by looking at the visible world. The fascinating beauty of certain reptiles and insects, of the monsters of the deep sea and of the microcosm (and some of the monstrosities of modern painting), may cause us to meditate on what the terrible and eternally new and revolutionary beauty of God might be like.

God also has a sense of humor: He is infinite Humor. We know the invisible perfection of God through the medium of the visible world: a green lizard, a rabbit, a grasshopper, a protozoön, a "praying mantis"* with its enormously long legs, kneeling on the ground as though engaged in silent prayer, may cause us to meditate on the infinite grace and the infinite inventive humor of God.

God is not only infinitely great but, as Dionysius the Areopagite wrote, "God is also small," infinitely small. And as, when we look through a telescope we can contemplate the image of God's infinite greatness, so, when we look through a microscope, we can discover God's infinite smallness. As the starry sky or the sea proclaim the majesty of God, so the eye of an insect or the digestive apparatus of an ant proclaim His humbleness. For if we can say that God is greater than the entire universe, we can also say that God is smaller than an electron.

"Everything you say of Him is wrong," wrote Meister Eckart.

---

* Literally, a seer, a prophet, but also an elongated insect of the mantidae family.—*Translator.*

SOMETIMES we feel God's eyes fixed upon us, firmly looking at us with infinite intensity, fixed upon us from all eternity. At other times we experience our soul looking at Him, widely opening its eyes, our entire soul concentrated in our gaze, transformed into this vision, and our vision and His become one, as though He Himself were alive in the pupils of our eyes, the lover and the Beloved merged in one single glance. At still other times the tiny soul feels the embrace of the Beloved, and it is all open arms, ready to embrace Him. Sometimes the soul embraces only the air, but at other times it feels the touch of the Beloved unmistakably. Sometimes a very subtle caress of skin and soul is experienced, causing a shiver in both (for what is the soul, after all, if not the body?). Sometimes the soul sighs, its entire being turned into a sigh, loving with a love that permeates its every heart-beat, inhaling and exhaling, while all the cells, glands and bodily organs, like a rising and diminishing flame, are in a continuous rhythmical movement.

The soul is like a woman, and sometimes it becomes a little coquettish in the presence of the Lord; it knows that it is loved, and it is conscious of its own charms and its power over the Beloved, and at times it even acts a little tyrannically, being conscious of His affection and of the soul's domineering role, but at the same time conscious also of its own total submission to His rule.

At night the soul sleeps smilingly and confidently, knowing

itself loved and tenderly caressed by the Beloved, cradled in His arms. Sometimes it awakes during the night, feeling His loving embrace and seeing a face delineated very close to her own: the faint outline of the veil of Veronica.

Today I have been looking at You with moist and sad eyes, the hungry eyes with which my soul looks upon the Source from which derive the beauty and gracefulness of all the maidens, the Source of the life of Ana Maria and of Claudia, of Sylvia and Miriam and of all the others, the Creator of their hair and their eyes, of their smiles and their dresses, the Source of all the other beauties of the world which mirror Your Beauty and of all the other loves which mirror Your Love. The eyes of the one who loves are then illumined by the vision of the Beloved, comparable to the love of a pair of small birds and the loves of all human beings and all animals. You and I alone are in this chapel, while outside on the highway the cars of the world are passing, and in such moments I am without anything and anyone. In such moments I am detached from everything and am alone in the universe. And yet, I have everything, I am happy and have no needs and no desires. For that which the others seek in women, in families, in friends, in festivities, I have right here. What the poet seeks in poetry and the painter in his paintings, I have right here. What the dictator seeks in power and the rich man in money and the drunkard in wine, and all that which in earlier years I, too, sought in vain, I have it all right here. Here is my entire life, my entire world, and all my loves. I own all of these riches, I who possess nothing. And I have all the joy, all the peace, all the beauty and all the loves. And I am satisfied with it all and desire nothing else. I possess You and in You I possess all because You are the Lord of all the stars, all the nations, all the landscapes and all the beings of this earth.

My liver, my brain, my heart, all the organs and glands of my body are here to love You. All things in the universe: poetry, the beauty of all maidens, of all the landscapes, all wines, all friendships, all days and all nights were created for the sake of my love for You.

All was created so that I might love You with the total capacity of my affection, with all my intellect and imagination, with all the tenderness of which I am capable and with all the sensitivity and the poetic talents that have been given to me, so that I might love You with all my passions, my appetites and my violent emotions. But also with all my sweetness, with all the fervor and fire and the insatiable desire for possession that I once projected into my love of creatures. But creatures threatened to become my tyrants:

> My mother's sons turned their anger on me,
> they made me look after the vineyards.
> Had I only looked after my own!
> (Song of Songs 1, 6)

Suddenly the soul feels God's presence with such unquestionable certitude that it exclaims in fear and trembling, "You must be He who made heaven and earth!" And the soul wants to hide and flee from this presence, but it is unable to do so, and it is caught and trapped as between a sword and a wall; it finds itself surrounded on all sides, and there is no escape, since this presence invades the soul as it permeates heaven and earth, and the soul finds itself in the arms of God.

And thus the same soul that had pursued happiness all its life without ever being satisfied, that had chased after beauty and pleasure, after felicity and joy, always asking for more and more, is drowning now in a sea of inexhaustible delight, and in vain it tries to find the shore and the ocean floor. "Let it be enough," the soul cries out. "If You love me, don't give me more of this joy, for it is going to kill me!" The soul feels permeated by a sweetness so intense that it causes pain, unspeakable pain, like something that is bitter-sweet, infinitely bitter and simultaneously infinitely sweet. All of this may last but for a split-second and may never return throughout life, but once this second has passed, the soul discovers that all the beauty, all the gaiety and all joys of this earth have vanished; they now appear to the soul "like dirt," as the mystics have said (or, in St. Paul's language, like "faeces" [skybala]). Now the soul can no longer take joy in anything that is not God, and it begins to realize that its life henceforth will be a life of torment and of martyrdom, for the soul is now beside itself, filled with ecstatic rapture and with a yearning for what it has once tasted, and it is eager to undergo all sufferings and all torments, in the hope of being privileged to taste this presence a second time, if only for another moment, if only another drop of the same.

Friendships, wine, women, travels, festivities, all these have disappeared forever, and the soul will never again know any other bliss that could compare with the one it has experienced.

Every human being possesses a secret interior chamber. In the inwardness of each of us there is a bridal chamber, to which only the bridegroom has the key. We all carry within us that hidden inwardness, that locked-up room, that place which has been created for the sake of love, a true interior paradise, but most men do not know of its existence.

And this is why most men are inwardly empty, without love. For no human love, even though it be most ardent, can ever violate this inner sanctuary. It is the chamber where the wine is kept, the place of which the bride speaks in the Song of Songs: "He took me to that chamber where He kept the wine." The bridegroom outside is knocking at the door, as we read in the Book of Revelation: "See, I am at the door, calling; if someone hears my voice and opens the door, I shall enter, and I shall sup with him and he with me."

Every human being hears this call in the depth of his being. It is that plaintive voice which Nietzsche heard in his heart and which caused him pain and fear. It is the voice of the Song of Songs, which says:

> Open to me, my sister, my love,
> my dove, my perfect one,
> for my head is covered with dew,
> my locks with the frost of the night.

And the beloved answers from her bed:

> I have taken off my tunic.
> Am I to put it on again?
> I have bathed my feet.
> Am I to soil them again?

Most human beings have in their innermost self an empty bridal chamber. Sometimes in the silence of the night a sorrowful voice can be heard, and someone knocks at the door. However, the interior of most men presents a sad spectacle, while outside there may be laughter and festival mirth. But it may happen that they rise and go to answer the call which they have heard within.

Within yourself you carry an abundance of caresses, of presences and of love, and yet you are alone. If you would turn to your inner self, you would find them, but this you do not do, for you are afraid of the agony of having to renounce all things and even yourself, for the Beloved is calling from your innermost being, or rather from the depth of your own self, a depth that is so abysmal that it causes you to believe that it is entirely out of your reach. It is even deeper within you than your conscience and your dreams

To be alone frightens you. In the train, in the doctor's waiting room or wherever you may be, you are afraid of being alone, of finding yourself without a book or a journal to read and with nothing worth looking at or speaking of. And all the time your only concern is with external things, and your hair is covered with night frost.

Man has been created to love, to love above all things his Creator. And all the time that is not dedicated to this love is time lost.

Love is the one and only law that rules over the universe, a law that, as Dante said, moves the sun and all the other heavenly bodies. It is a law of cohesion that unites all things. The matter of which the universe was fashioned is love. Every substance in the universe exerts a gravitational force of attraction upon every other substance. The earth attracts the moon, and the sun attracts the earth, the moon and the other planets and all the stars of the firmament, even the most distant ones. And these stars in their turn attract the sun [i.e., the center of *our* planetary system] and the planets and the earth with everything contained in it, as well as all the other stars, with the identical but converse force of attraction. And every particle of matter in the universe attracts every other particle of matter. Even when two bodies are in an absolute vacuum, without any interconnection between them, they attract one another with great force. Love means being united, and love is the only true source of happiness. Every soul which God creates, He creates endowed with love. This was the reason for the boundless disquietude that filled Augustine's heart until finally he began to understand for Whom his heart yearned and Whom it loved.

God Himself is that intimate feeling of solitude and the consciousness of the existence of a partner, a consciousness with which all of us are born.

68

And God is within the soul. He is present in the realm of dreams, in the darkness of the unconscious, in the deep abyss of the human personality. He is present with that intimacy which communicates with no one, neither with one's spouse nor even with one's self. In this interiority is the bridal chamber of the Beloved. When this bridal chamber is empty, then there dwell within man only loneliness, fear, melancholy and a great disgust. You may have your coffers filled with money, own property and have large deposits in banks; your house may be filled with plentiful worldly goods, but you remain empty within. When you find yourself in this state of inner emptiness and without God, the icy wind of loneliness will begin to blow. Sometimes at night such a depressed soul, deprived for so long of divine caresses (and this may perhaps happen after a night passed in pleasures and festivities), suddenly wakes up, terrified by its total solitude. At other times the soul may wake up in the middle of the night and weep bitterly.

WHAT we regard as reality, the reality of which we get hold by means of our senses, resembles a motion picture in technicolor. It is real, but it has only the reality of a motion picture, and there exists a more real reality. No doubt love plays a role in motion pictures; they may move us not only to love but to tears, and they may make us forget that outside the theatre there is daylight and spring and genuine love, and that it is there where the voice of the Beloved calls in the springtime: "Come, my beloved, for the winter has passed."

However, this second kind of reality is not perceived by means of the senses but is experienced in the dark light of faith. This kind of reality resembles a current of light that runs unseen in electric wires. And the voice we hear is like those waves of silent music that are being transmitted in space over great distances.

We should like to hear God's voice clearly, but this is not the case. The reason why we do not hear it clearly is that He cannot speak clearly through our senses. His voice is unfathomably deep. It is deep, subtle and inscrutable. It seems to express the anguish that is lodged in that ground of being in which the soul has its roots. It is a voice sounding in the night, a voice that calls and calls. One can hear it, but one cannot identify it. We should like it to be as clear as daylight, but it is unfathomably dark and yet clear, but its clarity resembles the obscure waves of x-rays. And, like x-rays, it penetrates to the very bones.

The voice of the Beloved is existential rather than vocal. It causes no echo in the ears nor in the mind but resounds in much greater depth, in that ground where God dwells, that is, in the innermost depth of man. The call expresses displeasure and disappointment. It speaks not with words but with deeds, and it takes account of real circumstances and situations. Because this voice issues from beneath the surface of existence, it seems to lack clarity, for we usually live only in the most superficial layer of our selves, and there we communicate with each other by means of words. But this voice comes from the deep, for God dwells in the deep ground of being. His voice is a great stillness.

The call of God—our vocation—is twofold in its meaning. God calls us, telling us: "Come and follow me." It implies both arrival and departure, both finding and continuing search. For, as St. Gregory of Nyssa says, "To find God is to go on seeking Him." Thus God's call is a constant challenge, a call into the unknown, into adventure, into following Him into the darkness of the night and into solitude. It is an incessant call to go further and further. For God is dynamic rather than static, as dynamic as His creation, and to meet Him is to forge ahead forever. Thus the man whom God calls is asked to become an explorer; he is invited to plunge himself into adventure.

God's voice is like the voice of a bird that one hears in the night; it calls and calls. And one can hear the voice of another bird sounding from a great distance. The second voice comes nearer, while the first voice keeps on calling, but from an ever greater distance. The voice which follows the call comes still nearer, while the call of the first voice is being heard from even farther away. In the end both voices fade away into the night.

PLEASURE is a false god who tells us: give yourself wholeheartedly to me, and I shall satisfy all your craving. But this god will never be able to bring us fulfillment, because our soul is greater than pleasure. It will be content only with a pleasure that is infinite. We are like broken jugs. Nor will we ever be satisfied with finite beauty, and every beauty that is not the beauty of God is finite. "In every perfection I recognized a limit," the Psalmist exclaims. This explains that inner feeling of sadness, that painful sweetness which is evoked by all beautiful things.

Animals are satisfied with all created things and never desire more. Man, on the other hand, is satisfied only with that which is infinite.

Every natural instinct demands that it be reasonably satisfied, and every natural need makes the same demand. Man, however, is born with an instinct for the infinite, with an instinct for God, and that instinct, too, demands satisfaction. This is that "infinite thirst for the infinitely illusive" (*la sed de ilusiones infinita*) of which Darío* spoke.

Every attachment to creatures leads to disappointment, to a frustration which resembles the one felt by a dictator who is being deprived of his power. It is an attachment to something

---

* Rubén Darío (1867-1916) was a Latin American poet, a native of Nicaragua, who inaugurated several literary movements and exerted considerable influence with his literary symbolism.—*Translator*.

which is not ours to possess, something which we try to dominate and which is snatched away from us.

If one has once tasted God, one no longer has any longing for creaturely pleasures. Once you have been treated to a lavish banquet, you have only disgust for bread infested with worms, the same bread that you devoured greedily and with delight in the concentration camp.

The effulgence of truth, of reality and of authenticity that glistens in all beings and that is the cause of their attraction, is the effulgence of God (since He is the Truth, He is infinite splendor), and this sweet sheen of goodness which shines in all beings as well as the dazzling splendor of beauty which draws us to all things, they, too, are God's effulgence.

From Him all the stars and all the beautiful strands of hair in the world borrow their sheen. He is present in all things, setting them on fire without burning them, comparable to that fiery bush which Moses beheld.

In the presence of everything that is beautiful, as, for example, the beauty of a woman, one ought to think of the infinite Beauty of the Beloved, the Creator of every earthly beauty, and one ought to delight with disinterested pleasure in the praise and glory which this beauty renders to the Beloved. And one should not lust for this beauty and desire to steal it from the Beloved, since my Beloved exists for me as I exist for Him. Therefore be gladdened by all this beauty, since it is a hymn of glory and praise of your Beloved and also a hymn of glory in praise of you. For, to repeat, you exist for your Beloved, and your Beloved exists for you.

The earth is beautiful in every place, in Nicaragua no less than in Venice, in Kentucky no less than in the Sahara. All the sights of the world are beautiful: the sea, the desert, the woodlands and the forests, the vastness of the steppe, the lakes, the mountains, the tropics and the arctic. God surrounds us everywhere with beauty and poetry, placing within our reach through the media of our eyes and of all our bodily senses the visible beauty which He has created and which is a shining mirror of His Invisible Beauty.

All the earth is beautiful, and all its nooks and corners are filled with enchantment; all its beings are seductively enticing, but who will not gladly resist these seductive charms in order to possess You who are so much more than all of these? And if the earth appears to us so seductive, how much greater will be our fervor when we shall be granted to see You face to face?

Gladly would I walk to the ends of the world if I knew that I should encounter You there. However, You are not to be found at the ends of the world but rather within my own self.

You are within me, and in Your eyes are the eyes of all the women whom I have loved, and who have passionately loved me. In Your eyes are reflected all the loving glances which have met my eyes in the world. But Your eyes are firmly fixed on mine from all eternity; from all eternity they have been looking at me.

HE who loves God wishes to be alone. He feels like a man who is betrothed to a woman: both desire to be alone, so that no one may disturb their intimacy, for every other person is now like a stranger to them. This is the reason why all those who have experienced God's love withdraw into silence and solitude.

"The soul cannot live without love," wrote St. Catherine of Siena, and the man who does not love God, loves other things, because the love which one feels for God is the same love which formerly one has felt for other things. And when man comes to love God alone, he loves Him with the same love with which he formerly loved a thousand things, but now he loves Him with the great strength of a person who loves only one thing in the entire universe, with a love that is total and universal.

It is in the nature of love that another human being comes to dwell within one's self. One feels oneself part of another person, and that other person becomes a part of us. In love we are two, and yet the two are as one.

When we love, we feel inwardly assured that we are also being loved; we feel the presence of the person who loves us and smiles upon us. To love is the desire to be the other and the inward assurance of being the other, combined with the certainty that the other wants to be me and that therefore he and I are one. To love is to empty us of ourselves and to fill ourselves with the other. When one looks at the beloved, the entire soul vibrates in this glance. When one sighs, the entire soul pulsates in this sigh. One knows that one has become a union of two, and one therefore identifies in one's feeling with every pair of beings that one sees: a pair of lovers, a pair of clouds, a pair of doves in flight, a pair of stars.

Formerly my feeling of loneliness and my sighs in the night did not find an echo in anyone; they went out into empty space. I was all alone. But now my sigh meets with an echo, it is aimed at Someone who may hear it, Someone whom I can neither see nor hear in the darkness, but faintly an answering sigh reaches my ear; it seems to come from afar, but it actually comes from within myself, from more deeply within than my own voice.

You, my God, are this Someone. I understand Your love and that You forgive all my failings, for, as You Yourself, I too, was once enchanted with other loves, and I, too, know how to forgive seventy times seven loves. I know the nature of Your forgiveness because I know the psychology of a person in love. The loves of my earlier years have taught me what true love is like. I thus know the nature of Your love for me, since I, too, have loved many times before, and I, too, know therefore the passion and obsession that love is and what it means to be madly in love, to lose one's self for another. And You have lost Yourself for my sake, and You love me with a love that borders on madness.

You love me with all my weaknesses, with all my inherited and acquired shortcomings; You love me just as I am, with all my peculiarities and my constitutional temperament, my habits and my complexes. You love me just as I am.

My soul has remained open. Oh, my God, You Someone that I am not, You have the key to my self. You enter and leave according to Your pleasure.

"THE Kingdom of Heaven is like a king who prepared a marriage feast for his son ..."

Christ told us that there will be no marriages in heaven, that is to say, no marriages of individuals with one another, since there will be no more need for procreation (the Mystical Body will be complete), and there will therefore be only one single marriage: the Marriage Feast of the Lamb.

Sex is a symbol of divine love. It is both a symbol and a sacrament, and therefore every misuse of sex is a sacrilege. And, being a sacrament and a symbol, sex is something which transcends its material reality, something more than what it seems to be: it is a reality which points to a far superior reality. It is a sign and, as such, it signifies divine love. This is why a Carthusian monk once said that monks and hermits have renounced what happens at nuptials for that which a nuptial feast signifies and symbolizes.

The Song of Songs may well have been originally a poem of human love (it must originally have been based on a nuptial love song), but divine inspiration transformed it into a symbolization of divine love. For, as we have said, all sexual love is a symbol of divine love. As a matter of fact, every poet who celebrates his beloved in song, all the love poetry of the world, all human love (and even the non-rational love of animals, the fertilization process of plants and the cohesive force of inert matter) is a form and type of divine love.

Marriage has such enchantment and is something so divine for us because it is an image of the divine espousal.

To love God is to possess Him, and therefore to love God is to be wedded to Him.

It is commonly believed that there is a basic difference between a person's consecration to God and marriage, because most people are not aware of the fact that the consecration to God is a wedding, and that, as St. Bernard says, a person who loves God "is married."

The erotic life of the monk has been crucified and resurrected. It still exists, but it has undergone a transformation. The monk is pure passion and nothing but passion, without an admixture of anything that is not passion and the rapture of love.

In every human desire, in every human appetite, there is a great deal of energy, passion and fire. And this energy and this fire reach their greatest intensity when the soul wholly abandons itself, to desire henceforth only one thing and one love!

Passions, appetites, affections, instincts and all the many anxieties of the human heart are the fuel of the love of God. Actually, the entire human being is this kind of fuel. And the love with which God responds to the soul may be compared with the pouring of oil on fire.

When we feel that a person we love requites our love, this intensifies our own love. Nothing, in fact, incites our love more than the knowledge that the beloved returns our love, and any increase of love on the part of the beloved intensifies in turn the love that burns in ourselves. When our thoughts dwell on the person we love, this causes us to love all the more, and the more we love, the more our thoughts will be with that person, even to the point where we become one living flame of love.

All the cells of our body, all the particles of our being are, in a manner of speaking, "nuptial," because we have been created for a universal nuptial union. What Freud referred to as "libido" is the oil that feeds the lamps of the prudent virgins, who live in expectation of the bridegroom.

Santa Maria Magdalena de' Pazzi used to run through the corridors of her convent, crying out in her rapture of love: "Love! Love! Do you realize, my sisters, that Jesus is love, that He is mad with love?"

A person who at any time has been madly in love can easily understand the nature of divine love. Human love and divine love are essentially the same, differing only in their object. The life of a religious vocation is wholly centered in love.

The member of a religious order does not renounce God's creatures because he believes they are evil but, on the contrary, because they are good and beautiful. They are so good and so beautiful that they have caused the religious to fall in love with their Creator, for we recognize the beauty of the Creator in the beauty of His creatures. We have, in fact, no other way and means of recognizing His beauty.

If, then, we have deprived ourselves of human beauty and human love, we have not done so because we have failed to appreciate them but because they have kindled in us the love for God. Is it not God who invented sex, and is He not also the inventor of all tender caresses, the Creator of voluptuousness and of passion? As Isaiah tells us, the Creator of all things is not a sterile God:

> Am I to open the womb and not bring to birth?,
>   says Yahweh.
> Or I, who bring to birth, am I to close the womb?,
>   says your God.

God is eternally young and new. His works are always vernal, and the world is reborn every morning at daybreak as though it had just been created.

The dawn of every day is a new "Let there be light!" and has the freshness and novelty of that first dawn. God makes the elderly leap joyfully in the early morning, and He causes the doves to frolic and the mocking-birds to sing of that God "who is the joy of my youth." The innocence and the charm of young girls derive from Him, who is the fountainhead of both virginity and fertility. And His is the only love that never ages, and He is the only lover who is neither unfaithful nor mortal.

YOUTH is the suitable age for one's self-surrender to God, because it is the age of illusions and the age of love—the love of a man for a woman, the love of springtime and the love that is being celebrated in the Song of Songs; and self-surrender to God is a surrender of and in love. And the more dreams and illusions you have ("a thirst for an infinite number of illusions"), and the more you love that from which you detach yourself, the greater is your gift and the greater is what you receive in return, and the greater will be the reciprocal love. If a person is disappointed with life and disillusioned, what kind of life can he possibly offer? God favors and asks for youth, ardor, passion and dreams. He wills that you favor and ask for betrothal and matrimony, because His love is a nuptial love.

The Church as a whole is united with Christ by a marriage, and so is each individual soul, because in every soul the entire Church is united, as the whole body of Christ is in every host and also in the bodies of all Christians. In the cell of a hermit the entire militant, suffering and triumphant Church is present. In the solitude of each soul which enters into marriage with Christ, the whole Christ is present, and since all men are united in Christ, Christ and all men are present in this soul, that is to say, the entire Mystical Body of Christ or, in St. Augustine's words, "the whole Christ."

TRYING to find our way to the Creator, we are drawn toward creatures, like a moth that dashes against a window. For God's creation is as translucent as glass, and God's splendor is spread out over it.

Attracted by the beauty we see embodied in things, we move toward them without consciously being aware of the fact that things are only mirrors of divine beauty. And yet this divine beauty dwells in our innermost being. And thus, paradoxically, the more we propel ourselves toward beauty, the more we are being alienated from its source, for this beauty is present within ourselves and thus can be found only if we move in the opposite direction from where we seek and see it.

One cannot first unite oneself with God and afterwards detach oneself from all things: one must first leave behind all things, and then one will be united with God.

God cannot unite Himself with a soul unless and until the soul consents to this union, as a person in love cannot be united with his beloved, no matter how deep and intense his love may be, as long as the one he loves is in love with others. God unites Himself with the soul at the very moment the soul loves Him. The union follows automatically. A soul which leaves behind its love for creatures does not remain suspended in a void—there is no void—but rather comes to rest in the unfathomable abyss of God. And the soul is then automatically embraced by God.

As one cannot pour wine into a vessel unless it is first emptied, so the soul cannot be filled with God unless we first empty ourselves of all things.

But before one can receive the embrace of God, one must first pass through that painful separation that is the prerequisite for the detachment from all things. All the desires and appetites of the soul must take leave of all those things to which they are clinging tenaciously, recognizing their transiency, and only then will the arms of the soul be free to receive God's embrace.

Love always moves the one who loves toward union with the beloved, and this is why God, who loves the soul from all eternity, unites Himself with it immediately, without a moment's delay, as soon as there is no longer any obstacle that separates Him from the one He loves, the one who loves Him.

The soul's detaching itself from all things may proceed slowly, in the course of the passing years, or it may take place in an instant. God breaks into the soul violently the very moment He finds the soul abandoned and alone, terribly alone, detached from the entire created universe and suspended in a sort of empty space, between the created world and Him. The soul then finds itself flowing over with God, since, as St. John of the Cross tells us, there is no real vacuum in the universe, so that emptying oneself of all is to fill oneself with God. But if there is even one single attachment left in the soul, one single affective tie to anything that is not God, then God cannot enter into the soul. If there remains this one single affective attachment, then the tentacles of the soul will cling to this particular affection, because the soul cannot exist without embracing *some* good, and so the soul will not yet be sufficiently free to embrace God. Therefore one must first pass through the agony of being without anything, without any created thing, before being ready to fall into the arms of God. This means one will first have to die to oneself.

As long as the soul is not willing to give itself to God without any reservation, God will not give Himself unreservedly to the soul. Therefore a supreme sacrifice is demanded. But the reward is likewise of the highest kind: the soul, in exchange for the multitude of particular beautiful, finite and fleeting goods, receives absolute, infinite and eternal beauty.

The journey toward God may be compared with an interplanetary flight that will become more difficult in proportion to the ever increasing distance and the eventual liberation from the gravity of the earth. However, once the frontier of this field of gravity has been left behind, the flight becomes increasingly easy, and before long one finds oneself more and more attracted by the field of gravity of the other planet for which one is headed.

Nature is religious in its very essence. The star-studded firmament, for example, is one great supplication. The spirit of every landscape is a spirit of prayer, and so is the deep silence of solitary places.

The crickets and the stars speak to us of God, and what they are telling us is that they were created by God.

The entire cosmos aspires to a union with that God from whom it has gone forth. All things are dispersed in the world, outside of God, and they yearn to become one with each other. The law of love is the supreme physical and biological law of the universe and also the one and only moral law ("I give you a new commandment: love one another as I have loved you").

All the appetites and anxieties of man, his eating habits, his sexuality, his friendships, are one single appetite and one single anxiety to achieve union with one another and with the cosmos. This cosmic communion is realized only in Christ ("when I shall be lifted up, I will draw to me all things"). And when Christ will be reunited with the Father, we shall be reunited with Him. This cosmic homecoming is what Christ wanted to reveal to us in the parable of the Prodigal Son.

We have come from the heart of God and are as much a part of Him as the foetus is a part of the mother. And we all tend to return to Him as man tends to return to the maternal womb.

Meanwhile our soul calls for God as the orphaned calf wails

for his mother, as the cow lows, calling for her calf that was taken from her.

We are drawn toward God as the night-moth is attracted by a flame and as the fishes at night rise to the surface of the water, attracted by the torch of the fisherman who is waiting with his harpoon raised high, or as the deer is dazzled by the lamp of the hunter whose gun is aimed at its heart.

The soul is born in love, and when it opens its eyes it encounters everywhere the reflection of Him who is love, but it does not encounter Him whom it loves. This is why things inebriate the soul with love.

All things have an element of enchantment but also an element of disenchantment and disappointment. The enchantment derives from the fact that all things are reflections and images of God, and the disenchantment is due to the fact that they are *only* images and not the real reality. They are not God.

Nothing in the universe is ugly. There is only beauty or a relative lack of beauty, a relative lack of the divine sheen in certain particular things.

Beauty, joy and pleasure appear in beings in a diluted form, but all things are nonetheless bathed in and illumined by beauty in varying degrees, as though overlaid with a diffused light. God alone is Light in its purity; He is the focus of all that is lighted.

Things bear in themselves an element of beauty, beauty in greater or lesser degree, but they are not Beauty as such. God is the light that bathes all beautiful bodies, and there is nothing in Him that is not pure Beauty. This is why if one has once tasted God, every other beauty and every other pleasure seems to be insipid and deficient. Every delightful thing or being causes us to seek God, the source of all delight and all beauty.

All the beauty we see is like a tiny drop of water that spurs us on to look for its source, or like a vein of gold that causes us to look for the gold mine. The beauty of golden hair spurs us on to seek for the source of this beauty. We ask ourselves: where does this wonder originate and whence came these beings whom I love? How beautiful must You be, You who are the Fountainhead from whom all the women and everything else that I have loved have proceeded!

The smiles of young girls, the flowers, the fishes of the sea and the fleeting stars that have sprung from the bosom of God, possess only a temporally limited beauty: they shine for a moment, dazzling our vision, and then are submersed again in the bottomless abyss of Him who has created them. Why then should we go on chasing after these fleeting beauties, why should we not look for the inexhaustible source of beauty, that focus from which all these countless sparks of beauty emerge, sparkle and then disappear?

All things have their supreme reality in God. Everything that exists has its pre-eminent existence in God. The reality which we perceive is like so many shadows, compared with the reality that exists in God. The reality which we perceive is as unreal as a colored photograph when compared with the reality which it depicts.

A butterfly, the snow and the mountains mirror that divine perfection which exists in the highest degree pre-eminently in God. In Him exist the infinite archetypes of the butterfly, the snow and the mountains which we see on this earth. They are all part of God's essence and are therefore god-like. Here on earth all of these things are limited, finite, contingent and individualized, whereas in God butterfly, snow and mountains exist in an infinite convergence. And the archetypes of the butterfly and of the mountains converge in God into one, for they are all one in the same God, who is infinite and who therefore is everything in supereminence; they and God are one.

87

God resides in matter, notwithstanding the fact that He is infinitely different from matter and that matter is opaque and composed of course-grained atoms. The reflection of God's unique Beauty produces all the beauty that is dispersed in things and beings—in the blue sea, in the sea-gull, in beautiful women, in the beauty of the heron and the beauty of the green and tranquil tropical rivers which at nightfall wind their way under palm trees.

How must it feel to look at that Beauty itself, unveiled, face to face, no longer reflected in unruly matter, but in its plenitude in God? In Him you will see again the beauty which you have admired in the sea, in women, in the snow and in the flight of the heron, no longer dispersed in transitory and individualized reflections but concentrated in one Infinite Being.

This is what Dante meant when, in the last Canto of the *Divine Comedy,* he speaks of the dispersed leaves of the book of the universe that are united in one single volume by divine love.

And this is also that ray of light in which St. Benedict in his ecstatic vision saw the entire universe united.

The airplane which traverses the skyways and the car which travels on the highway, the forests, the flowers, young maidens, the whole divine comedy, including all existents, have their eternal existence in God. But in God things and beings are not diverse and individualized as they appear in their creaturely reality, but they form one single essence, the very essence of God: they are God. Here on earth all things appear separately: a flower, a love, a poem, a piece of music. But in God, flower, love, poetry and music are one infinite and pure act.

The contemplation of God is a recapitulation and synthesis of all creatures. But they all must die in order to return to their origin, to that Unity of all things which is God. And we must renounce even our own selves, which are parts of this totality, in order to return to the All. Only by dying to ourselves do we encounter our true identity, because our true identity is not in our ego but in the All. We are centered in God as are all other things and beings. To communicate with all things is to encounter our own selves, and to encounter our own selves is to unite ourselves with all things. To give ourselves is to discover ourselves, to lose ourselves is to save ourselves ("He who saves his soul will lose it, and he who loses his soul because he loves me, will save it"). We live in a universe full of paradoxes.

Our ego is a solitary place, and he who rejects suffering and defies death and refuses to give himself, but wants to retain his self, shuts himself out of that Unity of all things which is God ("If the grain of wheat does not die, it remains alone . . .").

As the soul of the artist is mirrored in a work of art, so God is mirrored in the innermost structure of things. Just go out into the countryside in the morning and pay attention to everything you observe around you, the fragrances, the colors and the songs, and you will find in everything an effulgence of God.

All things in nature wear a trademark, the trademark of God. The linear marks of an oyster-shell and the stripes of a zebra, the veins or grains of wood and the fibres of a dry leaf, the lines on the wing of a dragonfly and the tracks of the stars on a photographic plate, the skin of a panther and the cells of the epidermis on the petal of a lily, the structure of atoms and of galaxies: they all bear the fingerprints of God.

In everything that exists we recognize a certain *style,* a divine style, which reveals to us that everything has been created by the same artist. Everything shows multiplicity in unity. Everything is both diverse and individual, and every individual has its or his own way of being, it is this and no other, and yet there exist millions and millions like it, and this holds true of the smallest animals as of the stars.

Every thing and every being has its own peculiar kind of lineament, its marks and spots, its motes and stains, its veins or stripes: the caterpillar and a piece of ceramics, the chamelion, the paintings of Paul Klee and a Persian rug, the foam of ocean waves, the rock formations, the luminous stripes in a piece of

agate and the carpet of autumn leaves, a piece of wood, the shell
of foraminifera* and the skeleton of radiolarians.**

* *Foraminifera* are members of a family of small sea animals with calcareous shells.—*Translator.*

** *Radiolarians:* a class of rhizopods with a silicious skeleton.—*Translator.*

EVERYTHING thus bears the imprints of God's fingers and, as is the case with our own fingerprints, God's imprints show both similarity and difference, both unity and diversity. Every such imprint is the seal of the Trinity, the seal of a God who is One and Three, infinite multiplicity and unity in diversity.

Analogous to the God who created them, all existents are simultaneously one and many, from the galaxies to the electrons.

There exist no two caterpillars that are totally alike, and the same is true of two atoms and two stars, even though in the nightly sky they look alike. However, all existents are ultimately one, and it is the function of poetry to discover this universal pattern, this unity of design that is the mark of all created things. Poetry can make us see the unity of things in their diversity: the mountains leaping like rams and the hills leaping like little lambs . . . Your hair resembles goats which roam through the mountains of Galahad . . .

The choruses of the frogs and the crickets who sing in moon-lit nights, the voices, the songs and the murmurs of all the animals—the crowing of a cock in the distance, the lowing of a cow, the barking of a dog and all the other mysterious voices that we hear in the farmlands, are divine services much like the Office chanted in choir by monks; they are psalms sung in different languages, and they are prayers.

The birds in their songs are asking the Father to give them

their daily bread and are praying that His will be done on earth as in heaven; they bless His name, and all the other animals are praying the Paternoster in their own mode and manner.

Every work of art praises God and gives glory to Him. So do the stars which proclaim the glory of God in the heavens. Every true work of art is thus in a certain sense a prayer. And art need not be of a specifically religious nature to give glory to God, for all art is essentially religious.

God's sanctity manifests itself in everything, even in the clear eyes of pigs.

In nature everything is clean and pure: the sputum of a person suffering from pulmonary tuberculosis as much as the clear water of the Caribbean islands (and this is why St. Catherine of Genoa drank the pus from the wounds of the sick and why St. Louis, the King, kissed the sores of lepers). The herons are as clean and pure as the worms. All matter is lucid and saintly, because it has come from the hands of God. Everything is clean, except sin. Everything is pure, except the fallen nature of man. A landscape is pure, because it has neither the appetites nor the disorderly desires of fallen man. All the animals are pure, because they know neither pride nor lust. And when a man is a saint, when he no longer has disorderly appetites and inclinations, neither pride nor lust, then his rational soul becomes as pure as the forests, the lakes, the worms and the herons.

An animal or a tree is a precise image of an idea in the mind of God (by this we mean God's very essence, since everything that has its being in Him is of His essence), and it is a true message, conveying without any possible equivocation exactly what God wants to convey in His message, nothing more and nothing less. Every material thing is an expression of perfect obedience. And everything makes manifest in its being what

God wants it to be. In the words of the prophet Baruch, all stars in the heavens answer: "Here we are!" And thus all non-rational things and beings are manifestations of the fulfilled will of God.

The human body, too, is sacred and saintly and incapable of sin, and thus where there is no will, there is no sin.

God's presence in all things brings it about that in our sins we are making God—who is infinite Innocence—an unseen witness, an unwilling accomplice as well as a victim of our sin. And this means piling sin upon sin.

To sin is to tyrannize God. But to sin is also to impose a tyranny on ourselves as well as upon God. A damned man is one who has perpetually imposed a tyrannical rule upon himself and who therefore has committed a great injustice to himself. To sin is not an exercise of our freedom but, on the contrary, the surrender of our freedom, and yet we make ourselves believe that in sinning we are making use of our freedom, not unlike those dictators whose propaganda screams that their dictatorship is "a government of the people." Many people believe that they are free when they do "as they please"; they are unaware that a dictatorship is lodged in their own selves; their will obeys this self-imposed dictatorship, and thus they actually do what they do not want to do, even though they nourish the illusion that this is what they want to do. This explains why they feel repentance for what they have done, since they have been doing what they did not want to do and since they really did not want to do what they have done. They believe they are free, because the dictatorship is lodged in their own being; they have set it up in the very center of their will and thus carry a tyrant inside, laboring under the illusion that they themselves are the tyrant, while in reality they are only slaves. But when it happens that such a man with an enslaved will rules over a nation, then we say that the people live under a dictatorship. The greed, arrogance, cruelty and hate which tyrannize the tyrant will then also tyrannize the people of such a land, and it is these vices which are then established in the offices of Prime Minister or President of a nation.

ADAM in Paradise was naked. Poverty, therefore, is the paradisiacal state. Adam was as poor as the animals, as poor as St. Francis of Assisi, as poor as Christ.

After the fall man can no longer be naked, but a monk's robe comes closest to an assimilation to the nakedness of Paradise.

Poverty is also closest to man's true condition, whereas riches are masquerades: we cover ourselves with external things in order to hide the nakedness of our true being. Falsehood and wealth are synonyms.

Wealth also falsifies things. A rich, fanciful dress, a lavishly furnished house falsifies the authenticity of the materials used, covering up the natural, naked simplicity of things by means of fraudulent devices.

In all poor things there is a certain lustre, the luminosity of reality. A gaudy, ornate object is always less real than one that shows forth simplicity. This is why Henry David Thoreau said that it was important for a man to be able and willing to go out into the street with patched trousers. The lustre of poor and simple things—things fashioned of clay, of straw, of coarse cloth, of unstained wood: things that are unpolished, raw, rough, rustic—is the lustre of naked matter and is comparable to the natural splendor of a naked body. And the same resplendent lustre is manifest in works of art, in their texture and in their colors.

If man had not lost his innocence, he would still go naked. We can see this verified in St. Francis of Assisi, whose only possessions were a pair of drawers, a sack and a rope, and sometimes he even did without these.

The untruthfulness of riches consists in confounding what one *has* with what one *is*. When a person *has* more, we believe that he *is* more. One may buy a car and then come to believe that the car has become part of oneself, as though the car were a part of one's body. This is why St. Augustine says that to deprive oneself of riches causes as much pain as to sever a member of one's body. When the people admire our car, we mistakenly think that they admire us. We tend to regard the things we possess as parts of our personality; we are not unlike mollusks which drag around a heavy load that is not part of themselves. In the same sense the possession of things falsifies our personality.

The rich man believes that what he *has* he *is*. He displays his possessions in order to arouse admiration, as though these possessions and he were one, which means that he wants to be appreciated for what he *has* rather than for what he *is*. The Roman poet Propertius was aware of the real worth of poverty when he took pride in having gained the love of a girl, not with his money, but with his poems.

Wealth is a fraud, and those who believe they can own a piece of earth on this planet, because they have a written document in their hands, are as foolish as those people in the United States who, because of some written documents handed to them by a fraudulent agency, are laying claim to territories on the moon. The birds and all other animals are at home in forest and field and derive great joy from their habitats, and the same is true of two people in love who are taking a walk in the forest, and of the hermit who spends his life in it. They are the real owners, not the person who has a legal title deed in his hands.

The latter possesses no more than some sheets of an official document, written in ugly juridical prose.

We own the whole of nature, all the earth, all the landscapes and the starlit firmament. And we lose this ownership if we narrow down our idea of property to a few hectares of earth. Only when we are poor can we possess the universe, as the birds, who are poor, own the heavens, and as the fishes, who are equally poor, own the water, and as St. Francis of Assisi owned all things. This is why St. Francis called poverty a great treasure ("we are not worthy of such a great treasure"), and he said that it is a great luxury to have one's meal while seated on a beautifully shaped rock, next to a spring and under an azure sky. The poor rich men, on the other hand, have to be satisfied with and elegant dining-room in a very crammed space.

We are sons of God, who is the Lord of all, and being His sons, we too are the lords of all the abundant riches of the world. We are surrounded by incalculable riches, and we need only reach out with our hands to take hold of them. A handful of clear water that drips from my fingers is worth no less than a handful of diamonds, and if we appreciate the water less, it is because there is such an abundance of it. A goldfish in a pond, a little frog, green-colored like jade, a smooth, shining pebble, a piece of wood that floats in the water, are real treasures, even though they possess no negotiable value in the stock-market.

He who buys a field and fences it in, robs himself of everything else. Religious poverty, therefore, does not mean to possess little but to possess nothing at all; it means to strip oneself totally of all possessions, in order to possess all. We are not satisfied with the legal possession of a few title deeds of property, for we know that nothing can be more our own than the air, the soil, the earth and the sky!

Poverty is also the virtue of the Holy Trinity, for the life in God is a communitarian and communistic life, and each of the Three Divine Persons gives Himself totally to the other two Persons, so that there is in all of them no "mine" and "thine," even though there surely is in them an "I" and a "Thou."

The fraudulent nature of wealth is also evident in the belief that material things can be embraced by something as spiritual as the human soul. In Nicaragua we have seen a dictator who was never satisfied with the lands he acquired, and the reason was that even though he had titles to these lands in the form of legal documents, the lands themselves remained as foreign to him as before, and thus his land-hunger remained unstilled. The green pastures with their cows and their trees and the river which passes through their midst, remained as inaccessible to him as before. He did indeed possess the titles to the land, but the land itself never belonged to him. Contrariwise, the man who goes out into the countryside to enjoy the beauty of the landscape or perhaps to fish in the river and who afterwards goes away without wishing for more, he, even though he is a poor man, has owned the land, but not the dictator who holds the deed of title.

Thus only by being without greed, only by being detached from everything can we possess all. This is why St. Paul says that he who owns something should behave as though he owned nothing; and that he who buys something should behave as though he had bought nothing; and that he who marries should be as though he were not married.

Money is a tyrant, and as Christ said in the language of His time, it is a "master" (a word which for the ancients conveyed the meaning "a god": "No one can serve two masters . . ."). And in the words which follow, Christ uses the name of the god of the Sidonians,* Mammon, because money is a false god, and to worship money is idolatory: "You either worship God or Mammon."

On another occasion Christ again compares the rule of money with totalitarian rule and with the worship of a false god: "Give to Caesar what is Caesar's, and give to God what belongs to God." With these words Christ did not intend to legitimatize the claims of Caesar (contrary to a frequent misinterpretation of these words), nor did he intend to convey the meaning that the things belonging to Caesar are on a par with the things which belong to God. The irony that lies in Christ's saying is obvious: it is not the money that belongs to Caesar, but on the coin that was shown to Christ was depicted the image of Caesar, and so Christ says that the money is Caesar's because it shows Caesar's image. What Christ really intended to say was that money is not our property but the property of Caesar, while we are the property of God. Thus the phrase "Give to Caesar what is Caesar's" means: "Leave the riches, the faeces, to Caesar." And the phrase "Give to God what is God's" means that we ought to give ourselves to God, because we belong to God, bearing His image in ourselves.

Money engenders tyranny, cruelty, arrogance and pride: it brings to mind the rule of Tiberius.** Every coin and every bill has the invisible effigy of Tiberius engraved upon it. This is why St. Francis forbade his Friars to touch any money.

The first commandment of the Decalogue, which enjoins us never to have any graven images, never to worship idols, may have been given primarily to primitive peoples who had not yet

---

* Sidon (in Hebrew and Phoenician, *Tsidon*) was the capital city of ancient Phoenicia, located at the site of modern Saida.—*Translator.*

** Tiberius Claudius Nero Caesar (42 B.C.-37 A.D.), Roman Emperor and dictator.—*Translator.*

outgrown polytheism; it may strike us as an archaeological relic, without any relevance for civilized man.

However, modern materialism is not very different from ancient polytheism, and the world has never worshipped as many idols as today. Cars, movie stars, political leaders, ideologies are the modern idols. The city streets and the highways are teeming with idols—the idols of commercial advertising and the idols of political propaganda, the smiling goddesses of fertility and material abundance, quack medicines and hygiene, the gods of beer, corn-flakes and dentifrices; the faces of dictators and political bosses and the somber deities of terror and war, of destruction and death.

And the same forces of nature which primitive man worshipped without understanding them, the might of thunder and the mystery of fire, modern man worships in electricity and atomic energy, likewise without comprehending their nature.

The whole of creation, from microcosm to macrocosm, reveals to us God's infinitude, and we ought to regard all things as symbols and images, as photographic replicas of God. They have no value of their own and should therefore not be possessed and enjoyed as though they were ends in themselves.

To possess God means to detach oneself from created things, and to detach oneself from things means to embrace God.

Only God can be truly possessed. If I see something and it pleases me, I may buy it, but this does not mean that I truly possess it. Even though I can give it away as a present or can sell it, I have not truly possessed it. Even though this particular thing will have remained inviolate, our faculty of possession has its seat so deeply in our innermost being that no external thing can ever penetrate to that depth. This explains the profound dissatisfaction that is experienced by all who are the proprietors of external goods, a dissatisfaction which they can never put to rest and that increases in direct proportion to the number of their possessions.

There remains something like an invisible wall of glass between us and external things, and the soul may beat again and again against that glass like a moth, without ever being able to get to the things themselves. And meanwhile the world outside goes on smiling at us, without ever growing weary.

The same holds true with respect to those persons whom we love: we can never possess them. They remain as inviolate in their deep inner being as we ourselves: we, too, remain undefiled. Even between husband and wife there remains a separation which is ever present, a personal inwardness which can never be dispelled. They can never be as totally assimilated as they would wish, and their dream of a total union is illusive.

God only can be truly and fully possessed, as He is the only one who has access to our interiority, to that personal inwardness where we can be both possessors and possessed. Only He has the key to our being.

The explanation is that God does not enter from the outside but from within, making fun of the moats and walls of our interior castle, using the secret passage ways of communication.

And we can unite ourselves with Him without taking leave of ourselves. More than that: we can unite ourselves with Him only if and when we dwell in the very center of our selves.

But you may ask: can we then never possess any of God's creatures? This thought would torment us through all eternity, because in all eternity we would never be able to forget them. On every occasion the memory of them would come alive again, and we should then eternally be tormented by something which we never truly possessed. The answer lies in the fact that we can indeed possess all things, but only in God. In possessing God we possess all, because He is the owner of all things. All things have come from God and will again return to God in Christ. "When I shall be lifted up, I shall draw all things to me," said Christ. And if and when all things will be drawn to Him, they will also be drawn to me, and He is more myself than I: it is He who is my deepest inwardness.

For Him, however, we must renounce all things. This is why St. John of the Cross says that the way to possess all is to abandon all our possessions, to disposses ourselves of everything.

And all the while we are like birds locked up in an apartment, striking against the window-glass of the livingroom. Before their eyes they can see a sea of light, without being able to get out of their prison. In a similar way we meet head-on with God's creatures, and we are mistaken about their identity because they resemble transparencies of God, and so we collide with them because they may offer concrete resistance and thus may inhibit our movement toward God. What passes through them unhindered is merely the sheen of God. And not until we forget the fascination with this creaturely light and turn back toward the darkness, shall we find the exit into the garden of delight, into freedom and light, the exit that leads into the open, into God.

WITH our eyes we can watch the dance of protons and electrons, performing a marvelous spectacle of configurations, like the color patterns of a kaleidoscope, but illusory like these, for they are only like colored marbles that glisten for a moment in the sunlight, the sunlight which is God.

This world is only an image, only a shadow. We remember that Plato spoke of shadows reflected on the wall of a subterranean cave; shadows reflected on the screen of a cinema or on the picture window of a television set, as we might say today.

And the stars in the heavens which smile and sing in the night are not so very different from those movie stars whom we see and hear singing and laughing on a screen, but who are not real but only the images of the singers, dancers and actors. And some of the stars we see in the night may even no longer exist, may have died millions of years ago, even though their light still reaches us, again not unlike some movie stars who have died some time ago but whom we can still see laughing and hear singing on the screen.

With our eyes, our ears and our touch we can perceive fleeting sensorial images on the screen of our senses, but these perceptions are not reality. Death will put an end to the spectrum of our life and will return us to reality. In the brief interim of our life we look at the world like children who sit in suspense, staring at televised pictures.

God, who is hidden in the dark, is reality, and we cannot apprehend Him with our senses, our imagination and our intellect. We can apprehend Him only in the dark light of faith, apart from our senses, our imagination and our intellect. For faith is not a real darkness but rather an invisible light which penetrates reality in a much greater depth than the one which is illumined by our sense perception. The light of faith resembles those x-rays which shine with a dark light.

God's presence is invisible and obscure, like the presence of another person in the darkness of our own home.

We have felt this presence within ourselves many times without realizing it, in the belief that we were alone with ourselves. This presence may make itself known by a sensation of total silence or by a mysterious feeling of love which wells up from the depth of our being.

Perhaps after the pleasures of a festival celebration, when in the dawn of day you return to your home and find yourself alone: in such moments of aloneness and quietude you may experience the presence of Someone, the presence of a saddened face close to your own, and yet not you. It is then that you may suddenly realize how empty you are. You are afraid to look at yourself in the mirror, because you know full well that what you will see is not really you, that your face is a mask you wear. And therefore you are as afraid to look at yourself face to face as if you had to look at a cadaver. And, being alone with yourself, it frightens you, and your fear is not very different from the fear that may overcome us when we look at an empty house.

You suddenly have the feeling that you, only you in the entire universe, are far away from God. While the galaxies, which slowly have been revolving on their axes for billions of years, and while the slow geological evolution of the earth and the abundant flora of the sea and the fauna of the earth have been obedient to God's law, you alone have been disobedient.

105

However, the Will of God, which you have failed to obey, is not something external to you, something imposed upon your own will from without, but rather something that is more yourself than your own will, a thou that is you, your most inward self, your true self-identity and the deepest willing of your being.

We also may feel the presence of the Beloved and His mysterious caress in the darkness. Someone is then present within ourselves, but we do not see Him. What we can and do see is only the material reality, a reality that is as unreal as colored motion pictures, as unreal as the commercials on television.

How often, even when I was far away from God, I could see in my dreams a turbid face, in hours of loneliness, in the silence of the night, after a day of festivity: what I saw was my rejection of God, whom I had relegated to my subconsciousness. But there it was, imprinted on the canvas of my soul, turbid and sorrowful like the face of Christ that was imprinted on the veil of Veronica. All my anxieties, all my dreams, all my terrible nightmares resembled this face on Veronica's veil.

God's love is lodged deeply within us; it draws us toward Him, toward the center of our selves, which is He. For love always seeks union, the union of love and beloved. Someone exists within me who is not myself. And we are made in such a way that God dwells in the center of our being, in such a way that to be centered in ourselves is to approach and approximate God. And yet we cannot reach Him, because the distance between Him and us is infinite: He is infinitely around us, above us and within us.

WE are living portraits of God, true works of art. Our deepest secret, the ultimate reason of our being, lies in the fact that we are not only ourselves but also images. Our essence does not consist in being ourselves but rather in being copies and photoprints of something and Someone else. And only when we reflect this totally Other are we truly ourselves. We are a white screen upon which God projects Himself. As soon as we remove the picture on the screen, nothing remains.

This mysterious duality is man's secret: something exists within ourselves which is All, and yet we ourselves are not nothing. We are a naught upon which the All projects itself. But we can blot out this All within us. And the soul in the state of sin is this kind of Naught.

On the one hand, we are sons of the Naught, and on the other hand we are the sons of God, for God created us out of nothing. And thus the Naught and God are the constituents of man's duality.

We have come forth from the heart of God, where, as parts of God, we had our dwelling place through all eternity, and this is the reason why we shall never be satisfied until we return to God. Meanwhile we are living in exile. We are temporarily sent into exile by God. And yet there can be no doubt that we have come from nothing, since as long as we were dwelling in God we were not ourselves, but we were God, and therefore being ourselves denotes that we are something that has been fashioned out of nothing. We were born from a chaos that was made fruitful by God. What the saints see when they look into themselves is that infinite naught and that chaos. But they look at the same time upon God, and the discrepancy which they see between themselves and God is the reason for their dreadful humility. They can see the naught within themselves, that is, a total insufficiency, a total emptiness, the very substance of disorder and decay of late autumn, death and oblivion. The material we are made of is that of late autumn and old age, a hunk of matter which fades away and dies, the material of which is fashioned a cadaver and everything else that is perishable.

The spectres of hunger, of pestilence and of the horrors of war give us some additional idea of what we are. And once we blot out the image of God that is projected upon us, we offer a spectacle of melancholy, anguish and death. Underneath every being there hides a cadaver and the ugly grimace of a corpse. In this shadowy zone of their existence men may still laugh, but their laughter resembles the grin of the dead in the freezers of a morgue. *This* is what frightens children in the darkness and what never ceases to terrify the child who is alive in all of us, in the darkness of the world of dreams, namely, the naught from which we have sprung and which we still are, the aboriginal dust that we were and to which some day we shall return and which we have never ceased being. The life that is within us is on the surface and fleeting. We are already dead in our dreams, and even when awake we are asleep and dead to a multitude of perceptions. The struggle of the artist is a struggle to preserve artificially this fleeting life of ours. And he who is in love struggles likewise to save his life from drab routine and death through the medium of his love. But everything wastes slowly away, and everything tends to submerse itself in immobility and death. Art, too, spends itself and tends to become merely rhetorical. Beauty ages and fades, and love, too, may turn into mere routine. And thus everything in the universe is subject to the second law of thermodynamics. Only God remains the living God, eternal Vitality, ever new and ever fresh, a perennial dawn. For only He is. He is Who He Is. He does not *have* life: He *is* Life.

"If any man is thirsty, let him come to me!

Let the man come and drink who believes in me!" As Scripture says: "From His breast shall flow fountains of living water" (John 7, 37–38).

EVERY event is a sacrament of God's will. As the body of Christ is hidden under the appearances of bread and wine, so the will of God is hidden under the appearances—the species—of daily happenings.

All the events of history are as sacred as the Sacred Scriptures, because they are just as much a manifestation of God's will. Even the seemingly most insignificant everyday event is an expression of the will of God and therefore as important as the most important event of history, whether it be a question of missing a train or a question of losing the battle of Waterloo.

And thus nothing in the world is either insignificant or irrelevant ("All the hairs of your head have been counted"). The seemingly most irrelevant event may bring about a basic change in the history of the world. The falling of a roof-tile caused the death of a Spanish king. And a child who today sells newspapers in the street may figure tomorrow in a story that fills eight columns in all the newspapers of the world. However, all the other seemingly irrelevant events in world history, even though we may not have been aware of it, have equally determined the history of the world. And the life of every human being is equally important, even though his name may never appear in newspaper headlines.

Our hidden daily life is filled with portent and mystery and looks like a prolongation of the years of the hidden life of Jesus in Nazareth, those years which, though they are not reported in the Gospels, are of no less importance than all those other events in the life of Jesus which are not reported in the Gospels and of which St. John says that "if they were all written down, they would fill the books of the entire world."

What we call Sacred History is only a fragment—illumined by the Holy Spirit—of Universal Sacred History, that is, of the intervention of God's will in the affairs of the world. All history is sacred, and so are the events of our own personal life. The Sacred Scriptures, from Genesis to Revelation, are an inspired sector of the totality of human events, from the beginning to the end of the world, from the first to the last dawn. The rest of the history of the world (and of other inhabited worlds, if they exist) has remained veiled in darkness and is thus a text that cannot be deciphered. However, the will of God is on that account no less present in this text.

But the text of world history may be changed by man, and man has indeed changed it quite radically, beginning with the first sin. Sacred History is thus also the history of God's will as it is being modified constantly by man. God has, for example, decided to lead Israel to the Promised Land. When the people rebel and want to return to Egypt, God changes His plans and decides to exterminate them and to create through Moses a new people. Then Moses implores God on behalf of the people of Israel, and God seems to change His plans once again: He is not going to exterminate them, but neither will He permit them to enter the Promised Land, as He had previously planned. "I swear that you shall not enter the land where I swore most solemnly to settle you" (Numbers 14, 30).

Thus the will of God is a most intricately woven texture that is constantly being modified by man's free will, but it is a texture

111

that is never undone. At every instant His will is changing, in accordance with the changes which the will of man effects in external circumstances.

In every particular instance the will of God takes into account the indefinite number of effects which follow from and which modify all the other happenings in the universe. When I pray for rain to benefit my crop or when I pray that the rain may be halted so that I may be able to accomplish some important task, I have present in my mind only the benefit that may accrue for me by the rain or by the cessation of the rain. But in God's mind are present simultaneously all the effects as well as all the consequences which the rain or the cessation of the rain will produce all over the world. Thus the will of God is a conjunction of His taking into account all these contingencies as in their combination they relate to God's infinite wisdom and infinite love. This is why we ought to accept joyfully everything that happens, for, no matter how calamitous it may today appear to us, it is all for our best.

The only thing that is adverse to us is sin, for sin is also the only thing that depends on us rather than on the will of God. Sin runs counter to God's will and is for this reason the only real calamity.

However, everything that does not depend on our own will, is the will of God. Even the effects and consequences of sin are the will of God, despite the fact that to sin or not to sin depended upon us, and the effects and consequences of the sins of our fellow men are likewise willed by God. A man's consent to his shooting of another human being depends entirely on him who does the killing, but whether or not the pistol was loaded and whether or not the cannon is fired, the trajectory of the bullet and whether it hits its mark or not, as well as all the other consequences that follow from the firing of the bullet or the cannon, depend on the will of God. This is why we ought to bless all that happens, since everything, even the effects of sin, is God's will. The only exception is our consent to sin.

Sometimes we do not wish to recognize God's will, because it appears to us in disguise or shows itself to us in very terrible aspects, as when the Jews did not want to acknowledge their King when the Roman magistrate presented Him to them with a crown of thorns, and they gave preference to the dictatorship of Tiberius: "We have no other king but Caesar!" The same Caesar who later on would crush them, while Christ was their liberator. We still give preference to Tiberius, who stands for power, pleasure, money, cruelty, and worldly glory. And we cry, "Crucify him. We have no other king but Caesar!"

The will of God may show itself in the disguise of cancer, or in a traffic accident, or in a totalitarian state, in the form of police agents, who come to arrest people in the dark of the night, and it is difficult to recognize and bless God when He appears in such disguises. However, all that which we call *reality* is an incarnation of the word of God and thus in a sense is also willed by God. And therefore all of reality is sacred. A chance meeting in the street, the train which you have missed and the airplane in which you travel, are all actualizations of God's will.

God is not only present in the form of the material species in the sacraments, but He is also present in some form or other in every grain of wheat, in every kind of wine and water and oil, and in all of reality. God is present in reality mutely, humbly and invisibly, and therefore reality as a whole is a sacrament.

We ourselves do not know what is good for us, and we should therefore desire nothing but what God wants or does not want for us, and we should accept all things in accordance with God's will, for only He knows what is good for us. We are surrounded by occurrences which we do not comprehend and of which we do not know whence they come or whither they go, pretty much like a blind person in the midst of big city traffic. And we are like a small child in the midst of a large airport, filled with airplanes that arrive and leave, and he cannot climb into the one he likes, because he does not know the travel route of any of them nor his own destination, and he must therefore wait until someone tells him into which plane to climb. Similarly, we ourselves do not know our destination nor what is the best route for us, nor which occurrences will harm or benefit us, because we do not know the future. And even the past and the present are known to us only partially.

It is sinful, however, to believe that one knows better than God what is good for us, that in some particular matter God may have failed us and be mistaken about us; that in some particular instance God may wish something for us which may be harmful.

Only God knows what is good for us, because all that happens and all that is going to happen, has happened in His mind from all eternity, not unlike a photographic picture that was taken some time ago and that we now see being developed in the darkroom, or like a movie that was filmed some time ago and that we see now projected on the screen, or like the light of a star that was emitted millions of years ago but that only now strikes our retina.

God knows that what is not good for me today may be good for me tomorrow. And God may not wish something today that He may wish at some future time; or He may wish something to happen at a particular place which He does not wish to happen at another place, or He may wish something for me that He does not wish for others. When Joan of Arc was

114

asked during her trial whether God loved the British, she answered: "God does not love the British in *France*." This answer hints at the mysterious vocation of us all. God may like a dictator who hails *from* Nicaragua, but He does not want him to be the dictator *of* Nicaragua.

WE live surrounded by miracles, but we do not realize it. Some of them are what is usually referred to as a miracle, but there are many others which we may call natural miracles. No one loves nature as much as God, the Creator of nature, and He wanted His miracles to be quite ordinary events. Being the cause of all causes, He prefers that all things have causes from which they proceed and that these causes produce certain effects and that all this happens in accordance with the laws of nature.

Everything that happens is in a sense miraculous, that which is ordinary as much that which we are used to calling "a miracle." As Walt Whitman says, a mouse is a miracle. Everything ordinary is miraculous, all the more so because it happens inadvertently. Such are the invisible and modest miracles of all our days.

This is why St. Augustine says that the miracle of the multiplication of loaves was not greater than the miracle that occurs daily with every seed. The only difference is that the multiplication of loaves was less "ordinary" or less "usual."

The act of creation was not an isolated act of God, an act remote in time, but creation is a perennial act that occurs before our eyes and the eyes of unbelievers at every moment, but those without faith do not believe even when they see it happen. We are being created at every instant, drawn out of nothingness at every moment. The entire universe is a perpetual miracle, and

116

the most common daily events are of the same order as the miracles of Lourdes.

It is precisely the ordinary that shows the manner in which God works miracles. Therefore, as we have said, the ordinary is as miraculous as the extraordinary. The only difference consists in the fact that we do not recognize the former as miraculous, for the simple reason that it is so very ordinary. However, for those who live in touch with God, life in its entirety is extraordinary, supernatural and full of miracles.

God works more palpable miracles than these daily ones in order to convince the world, but the inwardness of the soul does not stand in need of miracles that have to be verified by official legal records: He can work miracles by means of a mere coincidence of events in our daily lives.

Sometimes it is fairly easy to see the difference between a miracle and a mere coincidence of events, and occasionally mere coincidence can be genuinely miraculous, or God may work miracles by means of coincidence.

There really is no such thing as pure contingency. What we call contingency is but another name for the will of God. Sometimes it is difficult to recognize God's will, because it is incarnate in reality, in the laws of nature, in history, in the phenomena of physics, in accidents, in chance occurrences, in good or ill fortune, in fortuitousness, in all kinds of contingencies and coincidences, and all of these are manifestations of Divine Providence.

We are used to calling providential only what is extraordinary in our life and only what really or in our opinion benefits us. For example, we regard it as providential when we remain uninjured in a traffic accident or when we have not taken an airplane that was wrecked, but we are not aware of the fact that dying in an

117

accident or taking an airplane that is going to fall to the ground is equally providential. Actually, this mistaken idea of Providence is a remnant of Manichaeism, that is, of the belief that there exist two gods, a good god and an evil god, and that Providence symbolizes the triumph of the good god over the god of catastrophe and ruin. However, there exists only one God, and nothing in the universe escapes His providential rule, except sin. Everything that happens is providential, and all that happens is ultimately for our good, except sin. Only sin is outside of God's Providence, because sin is the only thing that is not made by God, but committed by man, although the effects and consequences of sin, which depend not on man but on God, are indeed providential. And thus both what is favorable and what is unfavorable to us, the ordinary as well as the extraordinary, that which happens and that which fails to happen, is providential.

Frequently, we do not recognize Providence because our will interferes with and opposes the will of God, and in this case we are taking our stand against Providence. If, on the other hand, we conform our will to the will of God and do not the least thing that runs counter to His plans, we shall see Divine Providence marvelously at work in our lives, and the unforeseen, the fortuitous and everything that happens from day to day, will be filled with meaning, and our entire life will be filled with blessed coincidences and miracles.

If in everything you fulfill God's will rather than your own, every encounter in the street, every telephone call, every letter you receive, will be full of meaning, and you will find out that everything has its good reason and obeys a providential design

Most men feel themselves alone and abandoned in the universe as though they were dependent exclusively on their own providential designs, as though they were creatures of their own making or creatures of chance, living in a universe ruled by chance. They feel themselves alone and unprotected in a hostile world, like children who have lost their way in a forest, rather than as beings who were created by God and placed by God into a benevolent universe, which itself was created by Him and for us. We surely are not alone, and He who has created us, lives within ourselves as well as outside and above ourselves. When in faith and with love we say "Our Father," even the vast interstallar and intergalactic spaces become friendly and familiar to us.

Once we become convinced that He who presides over the rotation of the stars, the galaxies and the vast expanse of the universe is the Same who also governs the rhythm of our blood, our metabolism and our most lowly daily occupations, we shall feel secure, confident and tranquil. He watches over the fire-flies as well as over the galaxies, and not one atom moves without His consent. What, then, is there to fear in the universe?

The physical laws of the universe and the moral law are one and the same law. The only difference lies in the fact that the moral law can be violated by man. We are unable to violate the laws of creation in thermodynamics, for example, but we can indeed violate the laws of creation in ourselves. Man is the only entity in the universe that is able to be disobedient. As long as we obey the will of God, we are in harmony with all the rest of the universe, and in this case we obey the same law to which all physical nature is obedient. For, as we are told by the prophet Baruch, all non-rational beings obey faithfully their Creator:

> He sends the light—and it goes,
> He recalls it—and tremblingly it obeys;
> The stars shine joyfully at their set times:

When He calls them, they answer, "Here we are";
They gladly shine for their Creator.

(Baruch 3, 33–35)

Joyfulness, too, can be a perfect prayer, because it is an act of confidence in God, and it testifies to the certainty that nothing evil can happen to us in the universe. At times joyfulness can even be heroic.

Sin is the desire of men to become gods: small, diminutive, finite gods, but gods nonetheless, or at least god-like. This means that man desires to be the hub of the universe, to be a law unto himself and to be his own lawgiver.

Sin is decreeing for ourselves a law of our own making and doing away with the Law of God. Sin, therefore, means establishing a tyranny and becoming a dictator of our own selves, for, as St. Bernard says, to disobey God is to become one's own tyrant. The damned man is doing a grave injustice to himself, for he has condemned his own innocent self to remain eternally separated from God, to become a naught, and God abhors the damned, because the damned is a man who abhors himself (for God never ceases to love the damned man with an infinite love).

God would gladly suffer the pains of hell in place of the damned, if God were capable of suffering, says St. Catherine of Siena.

God abhors the damned man because He loves him, and the condemned man is his own worst enemy. God loves what the condemned man is ontologically, or rather what he ought to be; He loves the potential and actual *being* that is incarnate in the condemned, but He abhors it when a man betrays his own being and becomes an anti-being. For sin is the denial of God and the desire to set oneself up as an anti-god, as a man-god.

Sin is something that is not, something that is an anti-existence. It is emptiness, a complete vacuum. It is something worse than nothing, for nothingness neither exists, nor is it sheer emptiness, whereas sin is a real naught, a living death. The damned man lives in an eternal state of death and is condemned to eternal *nothingness*.

Physical death is but a transformation of matter, but eternal death is matter in the state of an eternally petrified cadaver. It is, as it were, counter-matter and a counter-universe, the radical opposite of creation and creativity. Eternal death is the horrible grimace of a vital part of the cosmos turning into a cadaver.

A soul in the state of sin is like an extinguished star; it offers the frightful spectacle of an immense frozen and vacant universe in which there is nothing left but a vast desert. God is infinitely good and infinitely beautiful, and therefore sin, which is the absence of God, is also the infinite absence of goodness and beauty, and therefore infinitely horrible. If God is all beauty and infinite goodness, where God is not, where God is totally absent, there is nothing left but infinite horror. And if God is Absolute Being, sin, which is the denial of God, is bound to be non-being, total emptiness and the most horrible nothingness. The soul is a being, and it never ceases to be, but a soul in the state of sin, emptied of God, is a being that is absolutely empty and frozen, totally desolate and pure nothingness.

The fire of hell is also a fire of love. Hell, too, is the work of divine Love, said Dante. For in Inferno the souls still love, but they love without hope. Heaven is a love that finds a response, a love that can be possessed, whereas hell is a love that has turned into despair. In the Song of Songs we read that jealousy is as terrible as hell, and, as a matter of fact, hell and jealousy are synonyms. In hell, love is being rejected by the one who is loved, and thus hell is equivalent to a rejection of love. He who has experienced unrequited love has experienced a taste of hell on earth. Whereas heaven is the communion of saints, hell is total isolation and solitude, an ontological desert. The fire of hell is that same fire of concupiscence with which sometimes the flesh is inflamed here on earth—a selfish love and the fire of unsatisfied desire, of solitude and of jealousy. There is in hell a "material" fire, but we do not know what is its nature. However, we who live in the Atomic Age, have learned a little more about what its nature might possibly be. The eternal fire must resemble an eternal state of molecular and nuclear disintegration of matter. God is love and union, and His love is the force underlying the molecular cohesion of matter, whereas hell is eternal disintegration, matter that is split and dissolute in an internecine war and in the pain of self-hatred.

For us, death is not yet an existent. Our death occurred when we were baptized, and by means of baptism we share in Christ's death: we have died in Christ. Christ died for us, and He died in place of us, so that we might not have to die. Our physical death is but the beginning of eternal life, "the pre-condition of our resurrection," in the words of Athanasius. Those who have been baptized have already transcended death. Our physical death, therefore, is not a real death but rather symbolizes our meeting with Christ.

Christ is "the first-born among the dead," as St. Paul tells us. This means that Christ was the first (the first-born) also among the resurrected, the first one to pass through the shadows of death to a new life, and all the others will follow Him in due course, just as brothers, born of the same maternal womb, follow the first-born.

For a monk, for a religious, death is no more. Death is something that has been overcome. He who lives in union with God, fears nothing, for he knows that nothing can henceforth harm him.

While the world is primarily preoccupied with the brevity of life, for us religious this brevity of life and the swift passage of the days are our greatest joy. We look at the passage of time as upon a fast express train, and we are as joyful as the passengers on a train that travels toward a certain destination, headed toward a joyous encounter, for time is like a train that speeds toward its destination, a train that takes us to meet Someone.

It is a lie to say that life is short. Our life is not short; it is eternal. Ahead of us is not death but eternity. We were not born in order to die but in order to live, to live eternally. And so we do not lament the speed with which time passes, for life does not come to an end. What comes to an end is time, that is to say, that which is not, the steady change from future to past, from that which is not yet to that which is no longer; and what lies ahead is eternity, an everlasting present, without a future, without a past, without an end, a life that is present forever, eternal life. We do not fear death, because we are not going to die but rather shall pass on to a life that is more perfect, more true, more vital and, in short, more *life*.

We resemble the caterpillar which is asleep in its cocoon and subsequently undergoes a metamorphosis that changes it into a butterfly.

"I saw a new heaven and a new earth," St. John wrote in the Book of Revelation. The cosmos will not die, and there will be no "end" of the world but rather a total *renewal*. When we read in Scripture that the stars "will fall from the heavens," this means simply that there will be a new cosmos, a universe with a new and different structure. And in this new world there will be a new life.

We ourselves are part of this new cosmos, a cosmos that is still only in that state of gestation which precedes the new birth, a cosmos whose first seed is the body of the resurrected Christ ("the first-born among the dead" and "the first-fruit of the resurrection"). And this seed will grow and multiply to a point where it will take the place of the whole creation ("the Kingdom of Heaven is like a mustard seed . . ."). Matter will be reorganized in an "incorruptible" form, in a new structural, nuclear and cellular whole, and in the center of this new cosmos will be the body

125

of Christ, and the entire new creation will revolve around Him as the earth and the planets revolve around the sun: "And the city did not need the sun or the moon for light, since it was lit by the radiant glory of God, and the Lamb was a lighted torch for it" (Revelation 21, 23). When we commune with Christ, we commune with the resurrection and the renewal of the cosmos ("I am the Resurrection and the Life"). And then we shall drink from the fountain of eternal spring.

The cicadas which for a period of seventeen years remain buried in the earth as larvae and come to life in the spring to sing, symbolize the resurrection of Christ and our own resurrection. And every spring is such a resurrection symbol.

THE Christian lives the life of a traveler, says Clement of Alexandria. We are like tourists who are leaving their country, without suffering much from homesickness, because they are returning to their native land. We do not leave the world with sadness, like those who go into exile, but we feel great joy, like exiles who return home, like displaced persons who return to the land of their birth.

For those who do not live in hope for heaven, the pleasures and joys of life are sad, because they are bound to come to an end. Those who live in hope for heaven are the only ones who can fully enjoy the pleasures of this earth, because they see in them an anticipation of the joys that await them, and they are glad that they are wayfarers whose journey will soon end. They are glad because they desire that which is to come.

Now we see as in a mirror, but then we shall see face to face, and we shall know as we are known, says St. Paul. Now we are unable to see the mysterious essence of things, things as they are in themselves and as they are known and owned by God. All we perceive by means of our senses is the images of things, their form, their color, their savor, their touch, but these are not the things as they are in themselves and in their essence. What we perceive are the sensory reflections of things in our brain. And so we do see "as in a mirror." How will it be when we see "face to face?" Then we shall see the changes that are wrought in our friends, in all the things that surround us, in all things in the

127

world. Then, for the first time, we shall see not by means of sensory images but all things and beings as they are in the full splendor of their reality. Then we shall know them as they are known by God (for to know is to love, and to love is to know) and as we ourselves are known and loved by God. We shall know God as we are known by Him, for then we shall see God, too, "face to face" and no longer only "in a mirror," reflected in things. And as we shall see God face to face, so we shall see all things face to face, as they are seen by God, as they are in God, as they are.

We shall see beauty face to face, not the beauty which shines through in things and beings, but beauty as such, without the intermediary of things and beings. We shall see beauty itself rather than beautiful things, and we shall see it unveiled, simply and directly. Heaven is both, unending seeing and unending loving; to see will be to love, and to love will be to possess, and to possess will be to rejoice. We have tasted and tested the joys of this earth; some of them are greater than others, but all of them are the enjoyment that is derived from the possession of a thing. However, all things and beings are limited, and their enjoyment is proportioned to their size. The possession of God, on the other hand, is like an infinite sea of joy, unfathomable and never ending, like a jubilant and exultant shout that grows and grows in volume until it transcends by far our maximal capacity of joy.

We shall know as we are known. We shall possess God as we are possessed by Him; we shall own God as He owns us and we shall share in God's joy, and we shall be partakers of His Godhead. For to see God is to possess Him, and to possess God is to be like unto Him. "We shall be like Him, because we shall see Him as He really is" (1 John 3, 2).

And we shall then for the first time know each other, and

heaven will be an everlasting communion of love. For here on earth we can know each other only superficially, only, as it were, from the outside, and even those who learn to know each other better, even those who love each other, remain a deep mystery to one another and are in their depth two unknowns. We even remain unknown and mysterious to ourselves. Only in heaven shall we truly communicate with each other, only in heaven shall we be able to say to each other our most intimate word, without any need to express ourselves in spoken language, because we shall then live in a perfect communion of love. As we read in the Revelation of St. John, time will be no more. There will no longer be the torture of the passage of time, no festivity that is bound to end, and we shall no longer know each other only in the fragments of time, in the constant flux of the river of time, but rather with a knowledge that is total and complete, and in the everlasting presence of all those whom we love. The words we say and the speeches we make today are carried away by the wind; laughter disappears, and the joy of being together of those who love each other is constantly being scattered in the flight of time, as smoke is scattered by the wind. But then both space and time will be no more. We shall live eternally, in an eternal life, in a life that is movement, but a movement that has no end and is thus an eternal presence. Here on earth we can never stay united with those who love us, for if we want to be united with some, we have to be separated from others. And there are so many others whom we do not even know but whom we may also wish to embrace with our love, together with those whom we now love, even though at one time they were unknown strangers to us. But in heaven we shall all be united and shall enjoy the intimate companionship of all, of those whom we now know and love in an obscure manner as well as of all those whom we do not love because we do not know them. We shall then enjoy the intimacy of all of humanity, and it is difficult to imagine the fervor with which then those will love each other who even here, within the confines and contingencies of space and time, have been united in love and have enjoyed a mutual intimacy! We shall see again those who have died, those whom we have seen growing old and dying as well as those who have aged together with us. We shall see all of them again, and their bodies will then be so beautiful that no earthly body can compete with this kind of beauty. However, the beauty of the human body may give us some idea of what the splendor of the resurrection will be like, of what heaven is like. To touch a human body with one's fingers is, in the words of Novalis, like touching heaven. But beauty ages and, as St. Paul tells us, earthly beauty is in comparison with the beauty of the risen bodies what the seed is in comparison with the grown plant. What good, therefore, is money, success, pleasure, as compared with heaven? This is why we are not afraid of death but rather wish for it. And we do not lament the death of others but envy them, for we desire to follow them and to arrive at our destination as quickly as possible, and thus to grow old does not sadden us. We wish for an early death and want to grow old speedily, and we like the flight of time (and it flies indeed). We wish for a speedy end of space and time, for an end of earthly pleasures, for an end of bereavements, deceptions, anxieties, illnesses, for an end of death and the fear of dying.

God placed an angel with a fiery sword at the entrance of Paradise, and ever since there has been sadness and tedium admixed with every pleasure.

Ever since man was expelled from Paradise, he has been seeking what he had lost. Childhood, spring, the enchanting rediscovery of love are vestiges of the lost Paradise. And there has remained the innocence of animals, an innocence which, unlike man, they have never lost.

However, Paradise cannot be found in the tropics, as Columbus believed, nor in those "tropical paradises" which the travel bureaus advertise. It cannot be found in the springs of Florida nor at Miami Beach. Paradise is located on Golgatha. "This day you will be with me in Paradise." As the good thief said to Christ, referring to His Kingdom: "Remember me when you come into your Kingdom." And Christ, in His answer, uses the word "Paradise": "This day you will be with me in Paradise." By saying this Christ implied that He was opening again for man the portals of Paradise.

Christ in these words does not make use of a metaphor, for those moments when Christ in His agony was speaking to another man in the same agony, were not a time for speaking in metaphors. Those who have embraced the Cross and have climbed the way to Golgatha know perfectly well that there is no need for a metaphor.

From the time of Christ's agony and death Paradise has remained open again for man. But this Paradise is certainly not found in pleasure nor in the comfort of the tropical "paradises" of the plush hotels or at Miami Beach, but only on Golgatha.

Paradise means union with God. Eve springs forth once again from the opened side of Christ, as previously she came forth from the ribs of Adam. And once again Adam exclaims: "Yes, she is bone of my bones and flesh of my flesh. . . . Therefore man will leave his father and his mother and will be united with his spouse."

Man's union with God will engender a second time of transformation of this earth into Paradise. Where You and I are, there is Paradise, and all of nature is the beautiful scene of our union—the starry sky, the mountains, the blooming apple trees.

Nature is no longer hostile to him who lives in the presence of God. And man becomes as immune to every evil as Adam was in Paradise. But without God's presence, man feels surrounded by perils, and he knows that at any time things may wound him, crush him, suffocate, mutilate, bruise or cripple him. But he who lives in union with God knows that no leaf falls to the ground without His consent, that all the hairs of his head are counted and that no creature has the power to harm him.

For him who lives in union with God all things are transfigured as by a strange new light, and a spring of joy gushes forth from all things, even from the most ordinary things of daily life. All the moments of his life exude happiness, and there is a kind of magic charm, of subtle enchantment in everything that such a person touches or does. As Christ told the woman at the well, one must have the spring of living water in one's own interiority ("and the woman said to Him: Sir, give me of that water so that I shall thirst no more and shall not have to return to draw it").

Paradise is love. Every lover is conscious of the fact that he has lived in Paradise, if only for some fleeting moments, but he who lives in the love of God lives in Paradise forever.

Every human love is a glimpse of eternity, but this is an evanescent eternity. In this evanescence one experiences a faint glimmer of eternity, for the life of God is volatile, but it is an eternal volatility, an infinite present that never ends, while in human love we get hold for but a moment of an eternity that does not last. Human love is a short-lived eternity, whereas the happiness of God and in God is eternal volatility. God's eternity is not static, but it is Eternal Life, and He is the source of all life, and all life is dynamic.

As Bergson has told us, human love has borrowed the language of mystical love, and it was not mystical love that borrowed the language of human love.

In modern times marriage is regarded as a kind of mystical union, and the modern girl enters into marriage with expectations similar to the ones with which a Christian virgin approached her betrothal to Christ. Commercial advertising pictures domestic life as an earthly paradise. One entertains the hope and expectation that husband and wife resemble gods and goddesses, and it is for this reason that there is so much frustration in modern married life. One expects of creatures something which only God can give. One believes that a woman and a home can still an infinite thirst for love, a thirst which can be stilled only by God.

133

WE desire to be known. The tiny ants are happily at work, climbing up and down the stem of a plant, satisfied with the small bit of creation which God has given them and without desiring to be known or be famous, content with the creaturely anonymity in which God has created them, content with being what they are. God knows them, and that is enough. You, on the other hand, feel you live your life in "obscurity" and are not sufficiently known by the world, as though you were non-existent.

The spider which weaves its cobweb seeks no publicity. The small insect signs no autographs, but no movie star in all his (or her) glory is better dressed. And the Virginian nightingale flies swiftly through the woods, avoiding all publicity and trying to hide its beauty. And the rabbit, too, runs through the forest, trying to keep out of sight and happy with this kind of hidden life. You, on the other hand, do not wish to live this kind of an "obscure" existence, you want to be known!

No doubt to be known is to be, and this accounts for our thirst to be known (and if we are unknown, we feel like shadows). Eternal glory bears its name because it resembles human glory in that it, too, means to become known. But human glory is a deceptive glory, a deceptive kind of being, because it aspires to be known by human beings who, like we ourselves, have only a borrowed and shadowy existence, so that their knowing us does not affect our own being. Our value is not diminished by our living an obscure and unknown life, nor is our value increased by the fame we achieve with the aid of a publicity agent or because our names appear in the headlines of the press or because we are interviewed on radio and television.

Our true existence consists in being known by God, for to the degree that we are known by God, we are. Not being known by Him means not to be, for He knows *all that is*. Evil, however, God does not know, because He is infinitely innocent.

This is why St. Francis of Assisi repeatedly said: "I am nothing but what I am before God." And, according to Christ, God will say to those who are refused admission to the Kingdom of Heaven: "I know you not."

Our desire for fame has its origin in the fact that we are aware in an obscure manner that we do not fully exist unless we exist in the consciousness of Someone who is outside and beyond ourselves. And thus we feel that to be unknown is like not to be. To gain fame among men, however, does not make us immortal, for all men are mortal and have the identical need of being reflected in the consciousness of others in order to be; otherwise they are nothing but shadows. Our own reality, therefore, depends on other shadows, and we believe that we are real because we are reflected in the non-reality of others and are thus shadows of shadows. Therefore the glory of man is of the nature of a shadow.

Heaven, too, is a knowing: "I shall know as I am known," wrote St. Paul. Heaven is seeing, vision and contemplation. According to St. Augustine, our reward will be to see, for knowing, comprehending and apprehending means to possess (that is, "knowledge" in the biblical sense of the word), and it also means to love. Seeing is receiving, and as with our sight (and our other senses) we receive into ourselves all the perceptible reality that surrounds us, so to see God is to receive and possess Him. And to see God is also to be like God: "In the life of glory we shall be like God, because we shall see Him as He really is" (1 John 3, 2).

To contemplate God is to be like God, for man is an imitative being, and to see God is to aim at resembling Him. It is a continuing process of becoming more and more god-like through all eternity. This is why a soul that sees God *is* God.

The soul is essentially a mirror and therefore something that has no value of its own (as a mirror as such is only a looking-glass); it derives its value from the radiance of the beauty which it reflects. The beauty of the soul is the beauty of God as it is mirrored in the soul. And a soul without God is like a mirror without an image. It is therefore something that *is not*.

Man by his very nature is a thirst for knowledge, a thirst to know and to possess, and this thirst is a thirst for God.

To know God is what man seeks in his travels, in science, in books, in love. And this thirst for experience in depth is in all of us, and it will be stilled only when we see God. St. Thérèse of Lisieux was enraptured with heaven, thinking that there she was going to understand the true nature of birds, of the wind and of flowers. Knowing, knowing, and ever more knowing.

Then, however, we shall no longer know reality in a limited measure, through the intermediary of our five senses: we shall know reality in its totality, reality as it is in itself, by an immediate knowledge, with a "knowledge" of loving possession in the biblical sense of the term. In the words of César Vallejo, "There will be kisses of a kind unknown on this earth."

THE bees provide honey for man, and the silk-worms provide him with clothing, but the primary usefulness of plants and animals does not lie in the fact that they nourish or clothe man or in their being of service to other creatures which in turn serve man, but in that they transmit life to man and in their being his ancestors through the long chain of evolution. They are integral parts of man and are destined to share in the resurrection. The fossilized trilobites which lived five hundred million years ago, have not totally died out but have passed on their life to our own body and are thus in a sense still alive in our body, waiting jointly with us for the resurrection.

Man is in solidarity with all of creation, and when Adam sinned, he caused nature in its entirety to share in his corruption. "Accursed be the earth because of you," God told him. In like manner, when God sent the Flood, He not only regretted having created man but having created nature in its entirety: "I will rid the face of the earth of man, my own creation, and also of animals, reptiles and the birds of heaven; for I regret having made them." Then, as we read in Genesis, on man's account "the earth grew corrupt in God's sight, and filled with violence" and "corrupt were the ways of all flesh on earth" (Genesis 6, 7–12). And the Covenant established with Noah after the Flood and sealed by the bow in the clouds, was a covenant with all nature: "See, I establish my Covenant with you, and with your descendants after you; also with every living creature to be found with you"

(Genesis 9, 9–11). In like manner the new Covenant established with and by Christ embraced not only human beings but all creatures, and when Christ had risen, He told His apostles to preach the Good News to *all* creatures (not only to men). And all creatures groan with us in birth-pangs, waiting for the resurrection.

All earthly creatures are brotherly related by virtue of biological evolution, and the resurrection of our body is one more step, the ultimate step, of this evolution. And with the resurrection of Christ this final phase of evolution has already begun. Christ is the first exemplar of this new "biological" age of the earth or, in the words of St. Paul, "the first-born" and "the first-fruit of the resurrection." Our resurrection is like one more metamorphosis, and those metamorphoses, which represent earlier stages of life—from the Pre-Cambrian and Cambrian, the Silurian, the Devonian, the Paleozoic and the Mesozoic eras to our own—help us to understand this new and final transformation (St. Paul tells us that all we have to do is look at the metamorphosis of a grain of wheat).

Every birth is painful, for every birth is also a death. The coming forth of the child from the maternal womb marks the death of the child's comfortable foetal existence, and the child is being born crying. And all the stages of growth are so many other painful deaths which the individual has to undergo. "Unless a grain of wheat falls on the ground and dies, it remains only a single grain; but if it dies, it will yield a rich harvest" (John 12, 24). And unless a cell is subdivided, it remains only a single cell, but if it subdivides, it will yield rich fruit. The stars, too, are like grains of wheat; they, too, are being born into life through painful deaths; they owe their existence to gigantic explosions.

The entire cosmos resembles a grain of wheat and is like a

child in the maternal womb, in expectation of birth. This is why creation in its entirety groans in birth-throes.

The cosmic birth, too, is painful, and we resist it because we feel very comfortable, safely locked up in the smallness of our present cosmos, as though we were safely and securely in the darkness and warmth of a motherly womb, where we are allowed to sleep rather than live and where we have no desire to be born, to enter into a new life. But the process of life cannot be halted, and we have no other choice but either to pass on into this new life or to die. As Christ said to Nicodemus: "He who is not born again, cannot enter the Kingdom of God."

Christ is the first-born of this new birth ("the first-born among the dead"). The empty tomb of Resurrection Sunday was like a womb from which a first son was born. A certain quantity of our earthly matter (a quantity of calcium, iron, phosphorus or potassium) has already gone forth from this universe and forms part of a new creation. It has left a vacuum in the matter of our universe ever since the tomb was found empty on the Sunday of the Resurrection. And, as we read in the Communicantes (the prayers in remembrance of Christ and the Saints) of the Mass for the Feast of the Ascension: ever since "the substance of our frailty was placed at the right hand of your glory." The fragile biological substance of man was placed at the right hand of God; and we all are partakers of this frail biological human nature.

All this describes a natural biological process, as is clearly stated in the parable: "He also said: 'This is what the Kingdom of God is like. A man throws seed on the ground. Night and day, while he sleeps and when he is awake, the seed is sprouting and growing; how, he does not know. Of its own accord the land produces first the shoot, then the ear, then the full grain in the ear. And when the crop is ready, he loses no time; he starts to reap because the harvest time has come'" (Mark 4, 26–29).

And the harvest will be ready sooner than we believe. The prophet Amos tells us that in those days the man who still ploughs will already see at his side the one who reaps the harvest.

CHRIST has told us in many parables that the Kingdom of Heaven is a process of evolution: a grain of wheat, a seed which the sower goes out to sow in the field, a leaven which a woman mixes with the dough, the seed of a mustard tree which, when sown, is the smallest of all seeds but which, as it grows into a tree, surpasses in size and height all the shrubs, and in its branches nest the birds of heaven. Paul obviously used comparisons taken from nature and ordinary daily life, in order to make us understand that the Kingdom of Heaven evolves in a process that is analogous to the process of nature and the ordinary things of daily life. With these parables He intended to tell us that the Kingdom of Heaven evolves in a slow process, similar to the slowness with which the stars were formed over periods of billions upon billions of years, similar also to the formation of the earth, in the course of long geological stages—during extended periods of evolution in which the Kingdom of Heaven was already in a slow process of formation—and similar, finally, to the slow growth of a mustard tree and of wheat.

The cosmos is made up not only of space but also of time, or of a space that comprises time. When we raise our eyes to the stars, we see them not only through extended space but also through the extension of time. And when we look through a telescope and see the much more distant stars, we cause not only space but also time to recede, for we see things, the existence of which dates back many eons.

The dimension of time which we behold in the entire universe is like another parable of the Kingdom of Heaven. "If you only had as much faith as a mustard seed!", said Christ on another occasion. And we know that, as in a mustard seed is stored and locked up a mustard tree, so the entire chain of biological evolution was stored and locked up in the first cell. We are in possession of the seeds, seeds which are very small. But it is the nature of faith to clutch in one's hand a fistful of ugly, wrinkled and arid seeds . . .

There is hidden in these parables about the seeds an inscrutible mystery: the seeds are parts of the genealogical tree of evolution. We are descended from them or a gradual unfolding of them and, together with all other living beings of the kingdoms of animals and plants, we are constituent parts of the Tree of Life. The Kingdom of Heaven not only resembles a seed: it *is* a seed, and one primeval cell has been growing and replicating itself to assume the form of wheat, the form of the first mustard tree and eventually of man, in whose interiority is enshrined, as in a seed, the Kingdom of Heaven. And like the grain of wheat and the grain of mustard and the cell, which all in order to reproduce themselves, must divide, so man, too, must die in order to grow, to assume eventually the form of the whole man, the fulfilled man—the Mystical Body. Man must grow to a point where, as St. Paul says, the body of Christ attains to its full stature. In this Mystical Body are contained all living beings, our entire genealogical tree, as the birds of heaven nest in the crown of a mustard tree. For the Kingdom of Heaven is in the process of evolution and as such is a biological extension of the kingdoms of minerals, plants, and animals, as well as of the kingdom of man—a product of human socialization and hominization, to use the words of Teilhard de Chardin.

The Jews expected the Kingdom of Heaven to be an earthly

kingdom, and in this expectation they were not entirely wrong, because the Kingdom of Heaven is also an earthly kingdom: it is a heavenly kingdom founded on earth, and this is why we ask in the Our Father that the Kingdom of Heaven come to us. The Kingdom of Heaven is truly a kingdom or, as we might say today, a republic, a social order. The Kingdom of Heaven is a social kingdom, an *ecclesia,* a community, a spiritual kind of Marxism. Where the Jews were wrong (as wrong as today's Marxists) was in their belief that this new social order was to resemble the existing social order of this world, for as Christ told Pilate, His Kingdom is not of this world but represents a different kind of order. And to His apostles Christ said: "Among pagans it is the kings who lord it over them, and those who have authority over them are given the title Benefactor. This must not happen with you. No; the greatest among you must behave as if he were the lowliest, the leader as if he were the one who serves" (Luke 22, 25–26). In other words, the order is reversed. The Heavenly Kingdom is a kingdom without subordinates, a democratic kingdom, or a commonwealth of kings, as St. Peter says in his first epistle (2, 9). Isaiah had prophesied the coming of this kingdom, describing it as the new and true social order that men must make a reality here on earth: "The lion will live with the lamb, and the panther will lie down with the kid, calf and lion cub will feed together, and a little boy will lead them. The cow and the bear will make friends, and their young will lie down together. The lion will eat straw like the ox, the infant will play over the cobra's hole, and the young child will put his hand into the viper's lair" (Isaiah 11, 6–8). Christ came to this earth to establish this kingdom, a kingdom that is already realized in a limited measure in the communities of religious orders, in monasteries and, in a more artificial form, in scientific laboratories. In monasteries one is trying to work out the social

143

system of the future, but Christ came to establish His Kingdom not only in the experimental laboratories and in monasteries, but He came so that this kingdom might become a reality in villages and towns, in nations and in all humanity. The Church is humanity, and the present Church is the small and seemingly insignificant seed of this total humanity. This is why the Kingdom of Heaven is like a mustard seed.

And the Kingdom of Heaven, according to Christ's words, is like the father of a family, who produces things old and new. With this figure of speech and with the parable of the leaven and the new wine, He wants to tell us that the coming of the Kingdom is a natural process, the same process of renewal that occurs in all nature. It follows the vital law of conservation and revolution, of established order and new adventure and of that constant renewal we observe in all life: the seed that dies and is being reborn; in life and death and in the cycle of the seasons of the year.

WHEN you contemplate the vastness of the universe in a star-lit night (our own galaxy with its three hundred thousand million stars, and the stars which shine with a brightness of three hundred thousand suns, and the one hundred million galaxies in that part of the universe which is accessible to exploration), you ought not to be conscious of your own smallness and insignificance but rather of your grandeur. For the spirit of man is much greater than all these universes, because man can contemplate, comprehend and be conscious of all of these, whereas all these worlds cannot comprehend man. All these worlds are composed of simple molecules such as the hydrogen molecule, which consists of only a nucleus and an electron, whereas the human body consists of much more complex molecules and, in addition, possesses the gift of life, a life whose complexity transcends by far that of the molecular world. Man, moreover, possesses consciousness and love. And when a lover says that the eyes of his beloved shine more brightly than the stars, he is not using a hyperbole (even though the Dorado Sigma shines three hundred thousand times brighter than the sun), because in the eyes of the beloved is the sheen of understanding and love, a light which is not found in either the Lyra Alpha or in Antares. Although the radius of the universe measures one hundred thousand million light years, it has definite limits, and even the most inferior of men is greater than the entire material universe; he has a greatness of a different order, which surpasses any mere quantitative greatness. For the entire material universe circulates like a small point in the human intellect which speculates on it in its understanding.

And all these worlds are silent. They are praising God, but with an unknowing, mindless praise. But you, oh man, are the voice and the consciousness of these worlds. And while these worlds are incapable of love, you are matter aflame with love.

Your understanding, however, is not separated from all these worlds. You yourself are this immense universe, its conscience and its heart You yourself are a vast universe that thinks and loves.

According to Plato, the soul completes and perfects the universe and has been created to endow the cosmos with an intellect. Man represents the perfection of visible creation, and therefore we cannot regard him as of little worth and significance (as "a vile earth worm"), for to do so would be to regard as worthless and insignificant the entire work of God.

The vastness of the universe which you contemplate in a starlit night becomes even vaster when you look at yourself as part of this universe and when you begin to realize that it is you who are this universe, contemplating itself, a universe which, in addition to its spatio-temporal dimensions, acquires a new dimension of even greater magnitude within your own self.

We are the consciousness and the conscience of the cosmos. And the incarnation of the Word in a human body signifies its incarnation in the entire cosmos.

The entire cosmos is in communion. The calcium in our bodies is the same calcium that we find in the sea (and which we have drawn from the sea, for our life itself has had its origin in the sea), and both the calcium of our body and that of the sea derive from heaven, from the calcium that is contained in the stars and that floats in the interstellar oceans and from which have sprung the stars (for the stars are a condensation of the brittle matter of the interstellar spaces and derive from them as our body derives from the sea). Actually, there are no interstellar and intergalactic empty spaces, since the entire cosmos is one single material mass, more or less rarefied or condensed, and thus the entire cosmos forms one single body. The constitutive elements of the meteorites (such as calcium, iron, copper, phosphorus) that have split off from distant stars are the same elements which are found in our planet, in our bodies and in the interstellar spaces. Thus we are made of the matter of the stars or, to say it more accurately, the entire cosmos is made of our own flesh. And when the Word became flesh and dwelled among us, what Adam said to Eve became applicable to all nature: "This is flesh of my flesh and bone of my bones." In the body of Christ, as in our own body, is incarnate the entire creation.

In our body commune all living animals, all fossils, all metals and all the other elements of the universe. The sculptor who sculpts in stone consists of the same matter that is in the stone; he is, as it were, the consciousness and the conscience of the stone, the stone become artist, besouled matter. And when man loves God and enters into union with Him, the whole of creation, with its mineral, plant and animal kingdoms, loves God and enters into union with Him.

This is the reason why, for the Christian, nature is more sacred than it ever was for pagan pantheism. We are more than pantheists, for Christianity far transcends any kind of pantheism, and the Incarnation far transcends what any pantheistic philosopher could ever have dreamed of.

Our bodies are sacred. They are *Temples,* as St. Paul tells us (and for the Jews there was nothing more sacred than the Temple), and all matter partakes of the sanctity of our bodies. According to St. Gregory the Great, the entire creation is a

147

temple. For us, therefore, every tree, every stone, every lizard, every rabbit, all meteors, comets and stars are sacred and saintly.

Nature constantly communes with itself, feeding on itself and offering itself as food. In feeding and being fed, life communicates itself, and this "communion of life" is far from being "prosaic." It was the wish of the Creator that in order to live we should nourish ourselves by consuming other living beings, for He wanted all living beings to live in communion with one another. He did not want us to exist independent of other beings, to be self-sufficient but constantly to assimilate other living beings in ourselves and, by means of such assimilation, to be always in communion with the entire cosmos. The diatomea is consumed by the copepod, and the copepod is consumed by the herring; the herring is consumed by the calamary (the squid), and the calamary is consumed by the perch, and when the perch dies and disintegrates, it turns into inorganic residue which serves as nourishment for the diatomea or becomes an ingredient of human food, while the waste products and remains of man provide nourishment for the diatomea. In this way life and death are always closely interwoven, and life is always a being reborn from the same prime matter. It is therefore not very difficult for us to picture in our imagination the resurrection of the flesh of other beings and that their flesh is a derivative of still others. In all these transformations we see already actualized figuratively the resurrection of the flesh. With what kind of body shall we rise? We shall rise jointly with all bodies and all ages or, to express it differently and more accurately, what will rise is one single body, an incarnation of many ages and stages, a body in which we shall be the flesh of other beings and in which all shall form a oneness within otherness, as a foetus is inside the mother. Only those who are not saved shall remain cut off from this body, and for this reason damnation is a mutilation of the

Mystical Body. This is why St. Paul says that all creatures—plants and animals included—are groaning, waiting for the resurrection of our body. And therefore the resurrection of one single body heralds the resurrection of all bodies. And thus the resurrection of Christ—"the first-born among the dead"—suffices to bring about the resurrection of the entire creation.

Christ not only redeemed human nature but nature in its totality. Bread, wine and water, too, were redeemed, and all matter was consecrated and sacramentalized by Him. Even the birds and the fishes of the sea share in Christ's sanctity and in our own sanctity. Mother Nature was sanctified with the Virgin Mary, for we are all united in a holy communion, from the most humble invertebrate and mammal to the Mother of God, and even the humble mammal has a share in Mary's motherhood.

When we commune with Christ, the entire cosmos communes with Him. The Mayas believed that man was made of maize, for they were conscious of this communion and of this Mystical Body. And all the Mayan sacrifices as well as all pagan eucharists were like a veiled and imperfect participation in this cosmic communion, this Mystical Body (for, as Yahweh told the Jews through the mouth of the Prophet Malachi, He was the recipient of sacrifices not only from Israel but also of the pure sacrifices of all the pagan peoples of the earth: "From farthest east to farthest west my name is honored among the nations, and everywhere a sacrifice of incense is offered to my name, and a pure offering too, since my name is honored among the nations, says Yahweh Sabaoth" (Malachi 1, 11).

Christ chose bread and wine for the eucharistic meal, because these were the basic nutrients of the Mediterranean peoples, whose culture was at that time the most widespread, and bread and wine were the most universal food (and wheat is the cereal that is grown most widely on our planet). Thus the bread and wine of the eucharistic meal stand for all the fruits of the earth, of maize, cocoa, coffee, tobacco, of bananas, coconuts, chicha and pulque. And every fruit is like a synthesis of the cosmos, an assimilable piece of cosmic matter. Thus the bread and wine of the Mass are likewise a synthesis, standing for the entire cosmos. And they are a representation of our body, for our body, too, is a fruit: we are all the fruits combined and enfleshed. Our flesh and blood are bread and wine. And when bread and wine are transformed into the Body and Blood of Christ, they symbolize our body and our blood, transformed into the Body and Blood of Christ.

All beings share in the same cosmic rhythm. The whirling of the atoms, the circulation of our blood and the sap of plants, the tides of the ocean, the phases of the moon, the circular motion of the stars within their galaxy and the rotation of all the galaxies are all part of the same rhythmic movement, a choral chant sung by the entire cosmos. For, as we read in the Book of Wisdom, all the laws of nature are like the strings of a Psalter. The chant of the monks and the cycle of the liturgical year are in accord with the cycle of the harvest, the seasons of the year and the cycle of life and death (and in accord with the Life, Death and Resurrection of Christ). And thus the chanting of monks in choir is a participation of the human soul in the rhythm of the sea, of the moon, and the reproduction of animals and stars. The pagan liturgies, too, are in accord with the harvests and the seasons and make man a partaker of this cosmic rhythm, in a partnership which only the modern city dweller has lost. This cosmic rhythm is the rhythm of religion. As the oysters depend for their reproduction on the rhythm of the sea and as the palolos of the South Sea depend on the moon, so man depends on and stands in need of religious ritual and the cycle of the liturgical year. For, as we read in Ecclesiasticus, religion impresses its rhythm upon the life of man:

> Why is one day better than another,
> when each day's light throughout the year comes from
>   the sun?
> They have been differentiated in the mind of the Lord,
> who has diversified the seasons and the feasts.
>
> (Ecclesiasticus 33, 7–9)

This is why life in cities like New York is so horribly monotonous.

Our religion is Catholic, that is, universal, not only because it is the religion of all men but also because it is the religion of the entire cosmos. It embraces all, from the mollusks to the stars, and it has room for all other rituals and for whatever there was of true religion in all the ancient pagan cults. It comprises much more than what is meant by religion in the narrow and conventional sense of the term: it comprises the whole man, his poetry, his art, his folklore and his dances, the feasts of seed-time and the feasts of harvesting time, the growth of plants and animals and the love of man and woman, and apart from this religion there is no salvation.

The entire cosmos is a song, a choral chant, a festive song and a marriage feast (". . . a king prepared a wedding feast for his son"). We ourselves are not yet partakers of the feast, but we have been invited, and we see the light and hear the music in the distance. "At midnight there was a cry, 'The bridegroom is here! Go out and meet him'" (Matthew 25, 6). The Baptist had already announced his coming with the words,

> The bride is only for the bridegroom;
> and yet the bridegroom's friend,

151

who stands there and listens,
is glad when he hears the bridegroom's voice.

(John 3, 29)

The liturgy is the daily commemoration, on this earth and in time, of this wedding feast that was prepared in eternity. For the Catholic Church, therefore, all days are festive days, and in the liturgy all days are called *feria,* that is feast days (the feast of Monday, the feast of Tuesday, and so on), and all the days of the year of the zodiac and of the liturgical year are for us symbols of that eternal feast that never ends. And our song, joined with the choruses of the stars and the atoms, is the same song that is sung by the choir of angels, the same song that is sung perhaps by countless human species and by countless planets, a song to which reference is made in the Book of Job, when Job spoke of the joyful shouts of the morning stars which blend with the jubilant voices of the sons of God. We are now still far away in the dark, waiting for the bridegroom, but we can already see a light in the distance and hear a choral chant at midnight.